400

5/3

COUNTRY
CROSS-STITCH

McCall's Needlework & Crafts

COUNTRY CROSS-STITCH

McCall's Needlework & Crafts

MEREDITH® PRESS
New York

Dear Cross-Stitcher:

Meredith Press and the designers at *McCall's Needlework & Crafts* magazine have combined talents on this volume of truly singular cross-stitch projects. COUNTRY CROSS-STITCH is inbued with homespun flavor, whether traditional, floral, or celebratory. Because the projects are varied in design and difficulty, you can easily create gifts and home decorating accents that are personal and from the heart.

We at Meredith Press are dedicated to producing the highest quality craft books. We know that the straightforward instructions, dynamic photographs, and 2-color charts included herein will inspire you to some of your best cross-stitch accomplishments.

Sincerely,

Connie Schrader

The Editors

Meredith ® Press is an imprint of Meredith ® Books:

President, Book Group: Joseph J. Ward
Vice President. Editorial Director: Elizabeth P. Rice

For Meredith Press:

Executive Editor: Connie Schrader
Project Manager: Barbara Machtiger
Project Editor: Ellen Parlapiano
Editorial Assistants: Valerie Martone and Carolyn Mitchell
Production Manager: Bill Rose

ISBN: 0-696-02353-9 (hard cover)
ISBN: 0-696-02373-3 (trade paperback)
Library of Congress Card Number: 90-063670

Packaged by Rapid Transcript, a division of March Tenth, Inc.
Design by Stanley S. Drate/Folio Graphics Co., Inc.

Printed in the United States of America
10 9 8 7 6 5 4 3 2 1

CONTENTS

CROSS-STITCH BASICS

INTRODUCTION

Country cross-stitch. The very words evoke pleasant images of hand-stitched crafts with a cozy, heartwarming spirit. As you browse through the pages of this book those images will become a reality, and you'll find a number of inspiring country designs to work in the classic technique of cross-stitch embroidery.

Though the projects in this volume are as varied in style as they are in levels of difficulty, all are undeniably "country" in quality. You'll choose from five groups of projects that have been organized around certain themes. In the "Country Critters" chapter, for example, you'll discover ducks, geese, teddy bears, and other lovable creatures to stitch onto pillows and pictures.

The "Homespun Decorations" section features an assortment of folksy items for the home and includes pillows, plaques, and accent pieces that have been embellished with special messages, patchwork motifs, quick-stitch borders, and elegant monograms.

Old-fashioned crafts are the focus of the "Traditional Treasures" chapter, which showcases a historical sampler, a simple alphabet, and a striking ensemble of brightly colored pieces with the flavor of the Old World.

In the chapter called "Floral Fantasies," flowers blossom in an enchanting potpourri of botanical designs. Strawberries, roses, and a bouquet of other glorious garden delights grace samplers, pictures, pillows, and notepaper.

Finally, "Celebration Gifts" offers you ideas for one-of-a-kind presents to commemorate special events, such as weddings, births, and holidays.

The projects range from easy to complex, and whether you're a novice or an accomplished stitcher, you'll find many items to suit your level of skill. Even beginners can master the simple stitches required for the Quilt-Pattern Towel Borders, while such crafts as A Sampler Etched in History involve more time and experience. Many of the projects feature only cross-stitch, but a few combine this with other needle techniques. For instance, Patchwork Pillows from the Past utilizes both cross-stitching and machine-quilting skills; and the Flower-Twined Alphabet Sampler is first cross-stitched, then given the finishing touch with French knots, bullion, and satin stitches.

No matter which project you decide to try your hand at, the directions and accompanying charts are straightforward and easy to follow. If you should have a question about a certain embroidery stitch, the comprehensive section on cross-stitch basics will be a great help.

So choose your project, gather your materials, and start stitching one of these charming cross-stitched crafts. As gifts for friends, family members, or even yourself, they're all destined to become treasured country classics.

COUNTRY CRITTERS

You're sure to spot your favorite creatures in this menagerie of whimsical designs featuring animal friends from the barnyard, the forest, and even the toy box! You'll find graceful geese strutting across pastel pictures and sheep clad in coats of plaid, grazing in a matching wall hanging. Pairs of ducks are decked out in seasonal attire and posed on plump pillows. And for bear lovers young and old, a duo of easy-stitch pictures capture lovable teddies at rest and at play.

Barnyard Buddies to Frame

Muted pastel tones and Persian wool lend a soft touch to this trio of pictures cross-stitched on 11-count Aida cloth. A farm-fresh checkerboard motif surrounds the plaid sheep and ticking-stripe geese.

SIZES: Finished size, mounted but unframed, 12″ × 9″. Design area of each, 10⅜″ × 7″.

EQUIPMENT: Tapestry and embroidery needles. Straight pins. Scissors. Bright-colored sewing thread. Yellow pen or light-colored pencil. Embroidery hoop. Masking tape.

MATERIALS: For each: Ecru Aida cloth (11-count), one 12″ × 15″ rectangle. DMC Floralia Persian-type 3-ply yarn in colors listed in individual color keys; amounts, in yards, indicated in parentheses. Six-strand embroidery floss, small amounts of colors indicated in directions for individual items. Heavy white mat board, 9″ × 12″. Aleene's "Tacky" glue. Colorful narrow frames (9″ × 12″); refer to color photograph for frame colors.

DIRECTIONS: See "Cross-Stitch Basics," page 74. Prepare evenweave fabric. Mark center lines on fabric by folding in half vertically and horizontally, then basting with bright-colored sewing thread along center of thread groups in each row. Intersection of basting threads marks centermost thread group. Mark center lines on chart by coloring squares in rows indicated by arrows with yellow pen or light-colored pencil.

Place fabric in embroidery hoop, and referring to chart and directions for individual items, work each design as follows: Separate Persian yarn and work with 1 ply in needle. Begin where indicated in individual directions and work all cross-stitching. Solid lines on charts indicate backstitches. When cross-stitching has been completed, work backstitches (see page 76 for stitch details) using 2 strands of floss in color indicated. If desired, use the medium shade of floss to backstitch your initials in lower right corner, just inside border.

GOOSE AND GOSLINGS

Begin 1 thread group up and 3 thread groups to the right of center (bottom stitch of leftmost heart). For vertical dash lines along goose's head, neck, and body, use 1 ply of dark French blue Persian yarn in running stitch (see page 76 for stitch details). Backstitch goslings with light French blue floss, goose with dark French blue.

PAIR OF GEESE

Begin 4 thread groups down from exact center (posy above bow). Work vertical dash lines on geese in same manner as for Goose and Goslings picture. Use light French blue floss to backstitch outlines of geese and wings as shown.

PLAID SHEEP

Begin at 5th stitch below center (top of heart motif). For heavy diagonal lines on either side of heart motif, work half cross-stitch using 1 ply of moss green. Use 1 ply of dark brown tapestry yarn to backstitch ears; use rust floss for all other backstitching.

FINISHING: Remove work from hoop. Clip excess threads from back and remove basting threads. If necessary, wash piece as directed in "Cross-Stitch Basics," page 74. Cut mat board ⅛″ smaller all around than inside (rabbet) edge of frame. Center and stretch finished embroidery over board. Use pins to attach the 4 corners of the needlework to the mounting board. Place pins at centers of sides and gradually stretch piece into position until there are pins completely around picture and checkerboard borders are absolutely straight. Place glue along back of mat board and stretch excess fabric to back; use masking tape to secure until glue has dried. Insert mounted embroidery into frame.

PAIR OF GEESE	
◨	Dk. French Blue #7306 (1)
X	Med. French Blue #7304 (4)
O	Lt. French Blue #7694 (2)
·•	Pale French Blue #7301 (2)
◣	Rust #7176 (4)
•	Peach #7173 (8)
/	Camel #7421 (4)

GOOSE AND GOSLINGS	
◨	Dk. French Blue #7306 (1)
X	Med. French Blue #7304 (1)
O	Lt. French Blue #7694 (4)
·•	Pale French Blue #7301 (8)
◣	Rust #7176 (2)
•	Peach #7173 (4)
/	Camel #7421 (1)
—	White (2)

PAIR OF GEESE

GOOSE AND GOSLINGS

PLAID SHEEP

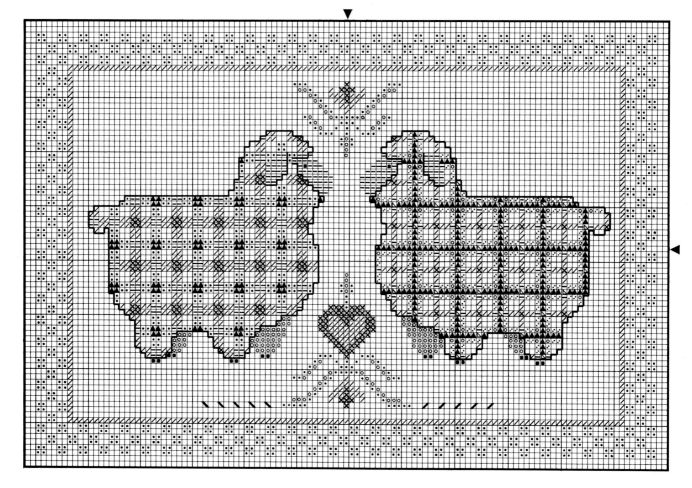

PLAID SHEEP

- ▲ Deep Moss Green #7385 (3)
- • Lt. Moss Green #7370 (8)
- ◘ Moss Green #7320 (2)
- ∴ Pale Moss Green #7369 (3)
- ╱ Peach #7173 (4)
- ▬ Camel #7421 (2)
- ◲ Brown #7457 (1)
- ■ Dk. Brown #7459 (1)

Just Ducky
Decorative Pillows

Even birds of a feather like to change their attire to suit the season, as evidenced by the dressed-up ducks on these throw pillows. Spring inspires a necklace of lavender blooms, while summer calls for a spray of yellow posies. In fall the ducks opt for blue-and-white bandannas; in winter they prefer a festive wreath of holiday greens.

SIZE: About 14″ × 15″ or 14″ × 16″, plus cording (designs vary slightly in size).

EQUIPMENT: Ruler. Straight pins. Scissors. Sewing and tapestry needles. Basting thread. Iron. Sewing machine with zipper foot.

MATERIALS: For each: 25-count cotton/rayon blend fabric (white for fall and summer pillows, pewter for spring and winter pillows), 18″ square piece. DMC 6-strand embroidery floss, one 8-meter skein of each color listed in individual color key unless otherwise indicated in parentheses. Backing and cording fabric (we used velour) 45″ wide, ½

yard. Matching sewing thread. Cable cord ½″ wide, 2 yards. Fiberfill.

DIRECTIONS: For each: Prepare as directed in "Cross-Stitch Basics," page 74. Baste across cloth in both directions to mark center of piece. Measure ⅝″ up along vertical line from center and mark position of first stitch with pin. Work design in cross-stitch, following chart and color key and beginning with stitch marked by arrow on chart. To work cross-stitch, cut floss into 18″ lengths. Separate floss and work with 2 strands in needle throughout. Fill in numbered areas with a single color, following key; also follow key to work symboled areas. Each square on chart represents a "square" of 2 horizontal and 2 vertical fabric threads. When moving from one area of design to another, be sure to count 2 threads for each blank square on chart. When all cross-stitching has been completed, work outlines and details in backstitch by following heavy lines on chart, using 1 strand of floss in needle, and working each stitch beside or between 2 cross-stitches. **Fall Ducks:** Outline border with dark blue and birds with tan floss; do not outline bandannas. **Spring Ducks:** Outline birds' bills and feet with dark gold, their bodies with medium gray. **Summer Ducks:** Outline birds with tan backstitching. Border: Work inner and outer "frames" by backstitching with medium orchid. Work lattice lines from lower left to upper right, alternating medium yellow, pink, and rose floss. Work remaining lattice lines from lower right to upper left, alternating orange, medium orchid, and light yellow floss. **Winter Ducks:** Outline birds with black, ribbon sections with bright red.

After backstitching, remove basting threads and press finished embroidery well on a padded surface.

ASSEMBLING: Measure 3½" out from border in each direction; trim away fabric beyond this point. Cut a piece of backing fabric to match pillow front. Make cording: Cut 2¾"-wide bias strips from remaining backing fabric, piecing as necessary, to make a strip about 2 yards long. Lay cable cord along center of strip on wrong side. Fold fabric over cord and stitch along length as close to cord as possible, using zipper foot on sewing machine. Pin and baste cording to right side of pillow front, placing raw edges of cording out and cording seam ⅝" from edges of pillow front; round corners slightly. Overlap cording ends ½" on bottom edge; trim off any excess. To join ends, cut off one end of cord ½" inside fabric cover; turn raw edge of fabric in ¼". Insert other end and slip-stitch folded edge over end. Stitch cording to pillow front. Pin pillow back to front, with right sides facing; stitch together with ⅝" seam, leaving an opening along one edge for turning. Turn to right side; stuff firmly with fiberfill. Turn in raw edges of opening and slip-stitch closed.

SPRING

1,	•	White (2)
2		Med. Gold #3046
	−	Lt. Orchid #3609
	▼	Dk. Orchid #3607
	∴	Lt. Olive #772
	●	Med. Olive #3347
	X	Dk. Olive #3345
	∨	Med. Gray #414
		Dk. Gold #3045
	—	Backstitching

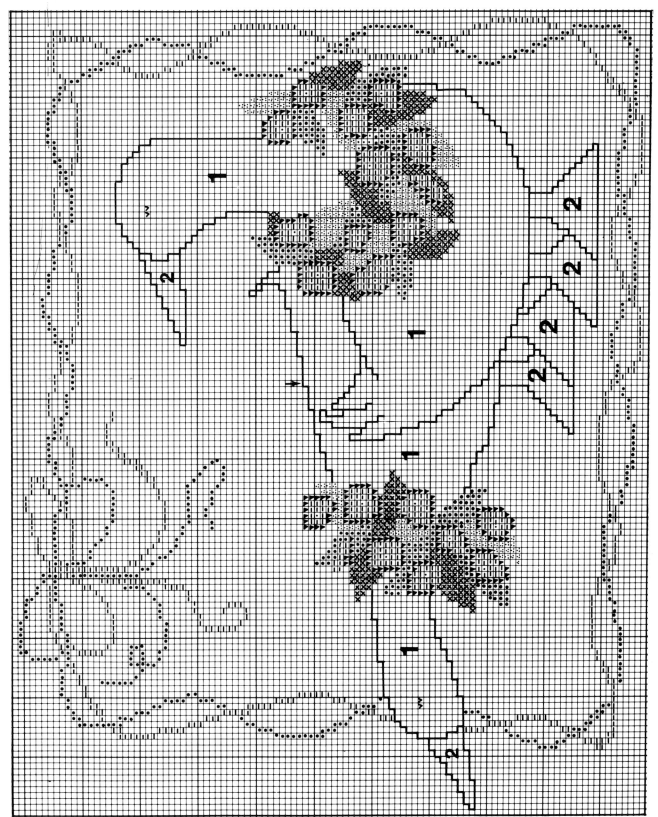

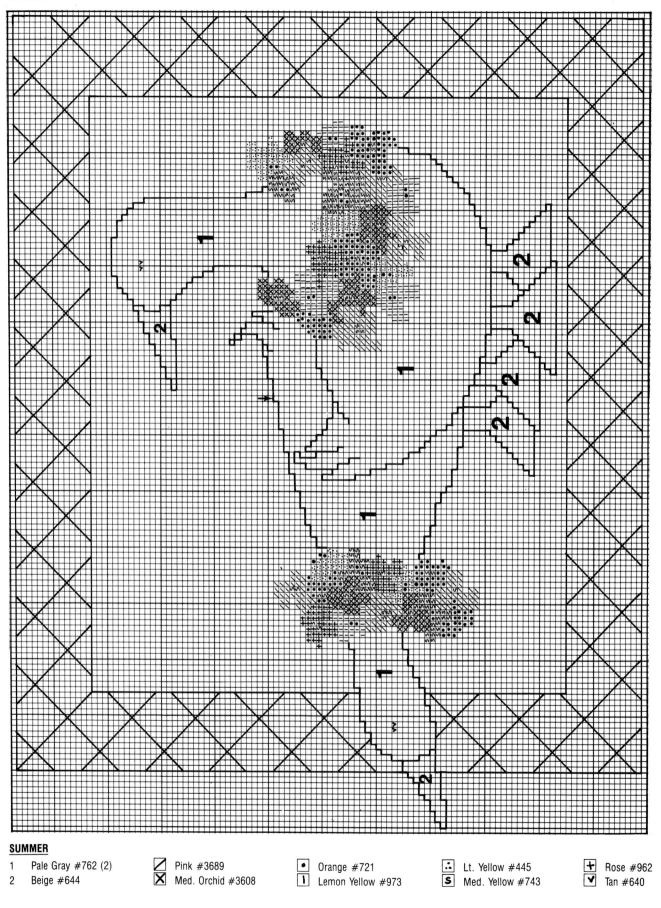

SUMMER

1	Pale Gray #762 (2)	◩	Pink #3689	⊡	Orange #721	⫶	Lt. Yellow #445	✚	Rose #962
2	Beige #644	☒	Med. Orchid #3608	Ꮖ	Lemon Yellow #973	ⓢ	Med. Yellow #743	☑	Tan #640

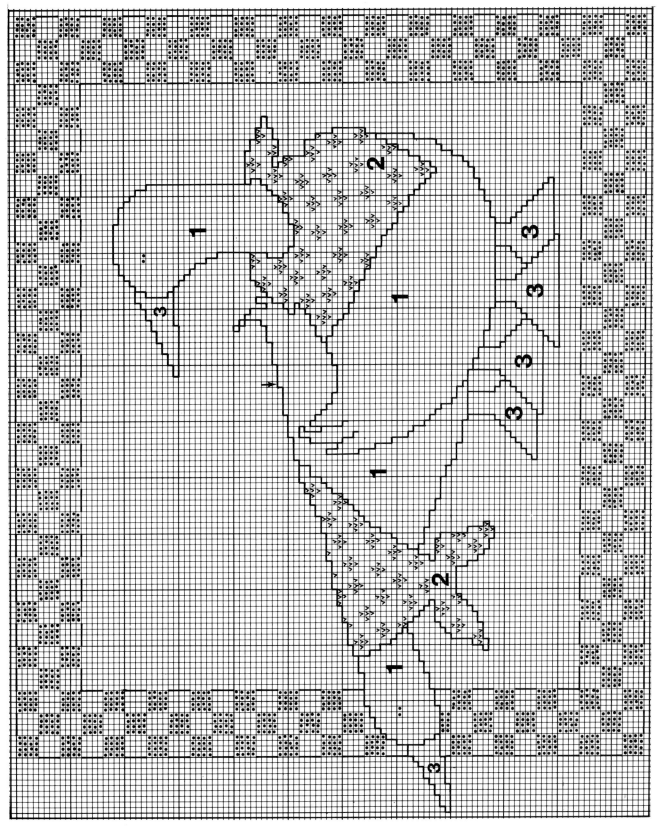

    1   Pale Gray #762 (2)   3   Beige #644

2, ● Dk. Blue #792   Tan #640

     ✔ Lt. Blue #794   — Backstitching

WINTER

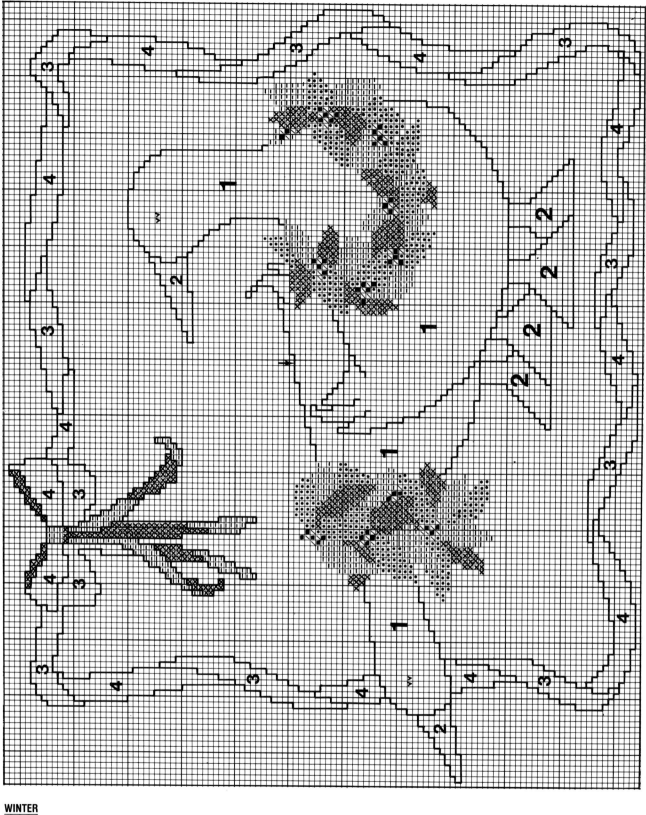

WINTER

1	White (2)	3,	✕ Dk. Green #986	■ Dk. Red #815
2	Med. Yellow #743	4,	⊟ Med. Green #905	╱ Brt. Red #666
☑	Black #310		• Dk. Bluish Green #909	

Beary Special Needlework Teddies

For the young, as well as the young at heart, these irresistible teddy bear pictures will bring a bit of whimsy to any room in the house.

SIZE: Each 11″ × 14″, unframed.

EQUIPMENT: Masking tape. Straight pins. Tapestry needle. Scissors. Embroidery hoop. Iron.

MATERIALS: Ecru Aida cloth (14-count), one 15″ square (ours has a printed bear border). DMC 6-strand embroidery floss, 1 skein of each color listed in color key.

DIRECTIONS: See "Cross-Stitch Basics," page 74. Tape fabric edges to prevent raveling. Following directions for individual items, locate first stitch and mark fabric square with pin. Place piece in embroidery hoop.

To work embroidery, follow chart and color key. Each square on chart represents 1 square of fabric threads; each symbol represents 1 cross-stitch.

Numbers indicate large areas to be filled in with a color. Using 2 strands of floss in needle and beginning with stitch indicated by arrow, work each cross-stitch over 1 fabric square. After cross-stitching has been completed, outline design areas and work details with backstitch, following heavy lines on chart; use 2 strands of black floss in needle (see page 76 for stitch details).

TEDDY BEARS' PICNIC

Measure 1¼″ in from right border and 3¼″ from top border; pin square for first stitch. After cross-stitching and backstitching, work grass blades in apple green with long straight stitches.

Bow-Tied Bears

Chart shows left half of design only. Fold fabric into quarters to find center; pin center square. Count 27 squares down from center, then 1 to the left; move pin to this square for first stitch. Work left half of design, using blue for bow tie. Follow chart in reverse to work right half of design, leaving 1 vertical row of background between bears. Use red for right bear's bow tie.

FINISHING: When all embroidery has been completed, remove fabric from embroidery hoop; remove tape from fabric edges. Gently press finished piece on a padded surface. Mount and frame as desired.

BOW-TIED BEARS

1	Cinnamon Brown #975
.·	Old Gold #976
╱	Lt. Gold #977
⌐	Black #310
◢	Golden Brown #435
S	Dk. Blue #995 or Red #666

TEDDY BEARS' PICNIC

	1	Brt. Yellow # 973
	2	Lt. Tan #738
V		Red #666
.·		Cerise #603
▲		Black #310
3,	◣	Dk. Blue #995
ω		Med. Blue #996
	4	Lt. Brown #434
	5	Honey Brown #437
8		Tan #436
+		Apple Green #704
	6	Deep Brown #801
⌐		Tangerine #947
I		Dk. Orange #740
⋏		Dk. Lavender #208
·		Lt. Lavender #210
●		Dk. Brown #938
S		Dk. Topaz #782

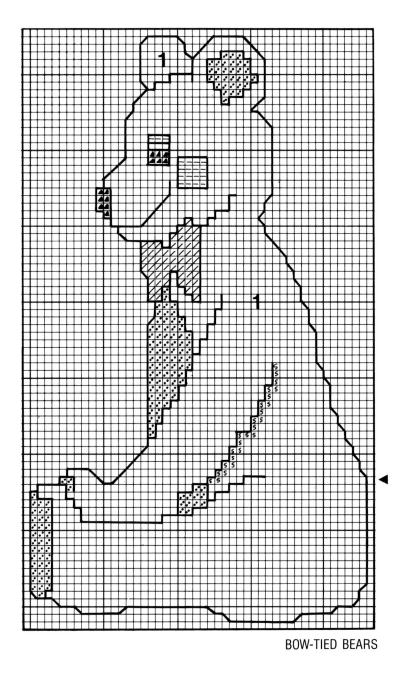

BOW-TIED BEARS

HOMESPUN DECORATIONS

There's no better way to show off your cross-stitching talent than by displaying these welcoming designs in your own home or by offering them as gifts to the special people in your life. Although they vary in style and complexity, each of these accessories will add comfort and an air of gracious hospitality to the home. Quick-stitch borders embellish pot holders and towels for the kitchen and bath, while pillow patterns work equally well in the bedroom, living room, family room, and any area that calls for a cushiony accent. There are also a number of message-bearing plaques, including one for city dwellers that celebrates the joys of apartment living.

Quilt-Pattern Towel Borders and a Plaque That Says "Welcome"

You don't have to be an experienced quilter to turn out patchwork designs. These traditional quilting motifs are cross-stitched on bath linens, hand towels, and borders for trimming baskets and other bath accessories. The coordinating picture bids a warm welcome to guests.

SIZES: Design areas for bath towel, 10″ × 3¼″; for hand towel, 12⅝″ × 2¾″; for huck towels, 12¾″ × 2⅝″ for one style, 9⅜″ × 2½″ for the other; for basket trim, ⅝″ wide and length as needed.

EQUIPMENT: Straight pins. Embroidery needles. Rubber cement.

MATERIALS: Bath towels from the Charles Craft Cross-Stitch Collectibles bath line: peach bath towel and hand towel; ivory Gourmet huck towels from Charles Craft* with 14-count Aida border. Small deep-toned basket. Ivory Ribband* (14-count) cross-stitch ribbon 1″ wide with scalloped edges, length as needed to surround basket plus ½″. Susan Bates/Anchor embroidery floss, 1 skein of each color listed in color key. (*See Source Guide, page 78.)

GENERAL DIRECTIONS: See "Cross-Stitch Basics," page 74. Fold Aida areas in half crosswise and lengthwise to locate center; mark fabric thread with a pin. Begin at center with stitch indicated by arrows on appropriate chart. Work cross-stitch design by following chart, color key, and directions

below; use 2 strands of floss throughout. Work each cross-stitch over 1 "square" of horizontal and vertical fabric threads.

BATH TOWEL

Work by following Chart A. Repeat motif on either side, once or twice as desired. When cross-stitching has been completed, work backstitches over 1 thread, using 2 strands of floss as indicated.

HAND TOWEL

Work by following Chart B. Work repeat motif once to the right, then follow repeat in reverse twice to the left of previously stitched design for a total of 5 framed motifs.

TEA TOWELS

Work cross-stitches by following Chart C or Chart D. Repeat entire chart once on either side.

Basket Trim

Work cross-stitches by following Chart E. Repeat entire motif on either side of center along entire length of ribbon. Use rubber cement to glue along rim of basket, neatly overlapping one end over the other.

Plaque That Says "Welcome"

SIZE: Design area, 5″ × 7″; framed, 9½ × 11½″.

EQUIPMENT: Straight pins. Embroidery needles. Embroidery hoop.

MATERIALS: Ecru Aida cloth (11-count), 9″ × 12″ piece. Susan Bates/Anchor 6-strand embroidery floss: 1 skein of each color listed in color key. Oval octagonal frame from Sunshine Station: style #8866-M, cherry finish (see Source Guide, page 78).

DIRECTIONS: Prepare Aida cloth as directed. Fold Aida in quarters to locate center; mark fabric thread with a pin. Place Aida with longer edges at sides. Place fabric in hoop.

Work design in cross-stitch, following chart and color key and beginning at pin with stitch indicated by arrows on chart. Use 3 strands of floss in needle and work each stitch over 1 "square" of horizontal and vertical fabric threads. When all cross-stitching has been completed, work backstitches over 1 fabric square as follows: Outline fence and gate posts using 3 strands of gray; work window panes using 2 strands of black; outline windows using 2 strands of dark brown; and outline house and eaves of roof using 1 strand of dark brown. Backstitch the lettering "to our home" using 4 strands of turquoise; work continuous lines over 1 or 2 fabric squares. Work French knots using 3 strands of floss; refer to color key for colors.

Mount and frame by following manufacturer's instructions.

Chart A
BATH TOWEL

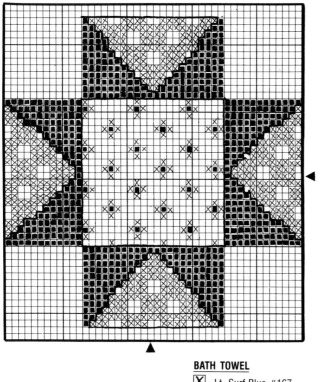

Chart D
TEA TOWEL

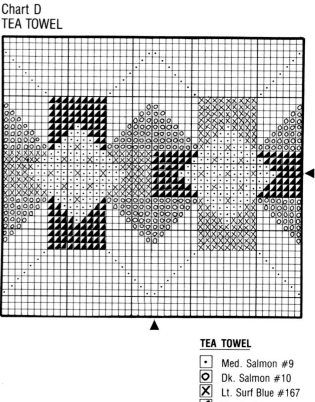

TEA TOWEL
- · Med. Salmon #9
- ⊙ Dk. Salmon #10
- ☒ Lt. Surf Blue #167
- ◣ Dk. Surf Blue #168

BATH TOWEL
- ☒ Lt. Surf Blue #167
- ▣ Dk. Terra-Cotta #341
- — Backstitch in Dk. Surf Blue #168

Chart C
TEA TOWEL

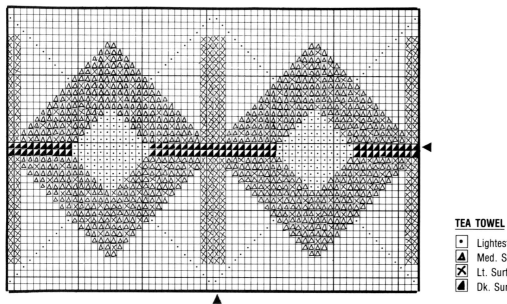

TEA TOWEL
- · Lightest Salmon #6
- ▲ Med. Salmon #9
- ☒ Lt. Surf Blue #167
- ◣ Dk. Surf Blue #168

PLAQUE THAT SAYS "WELCOME"

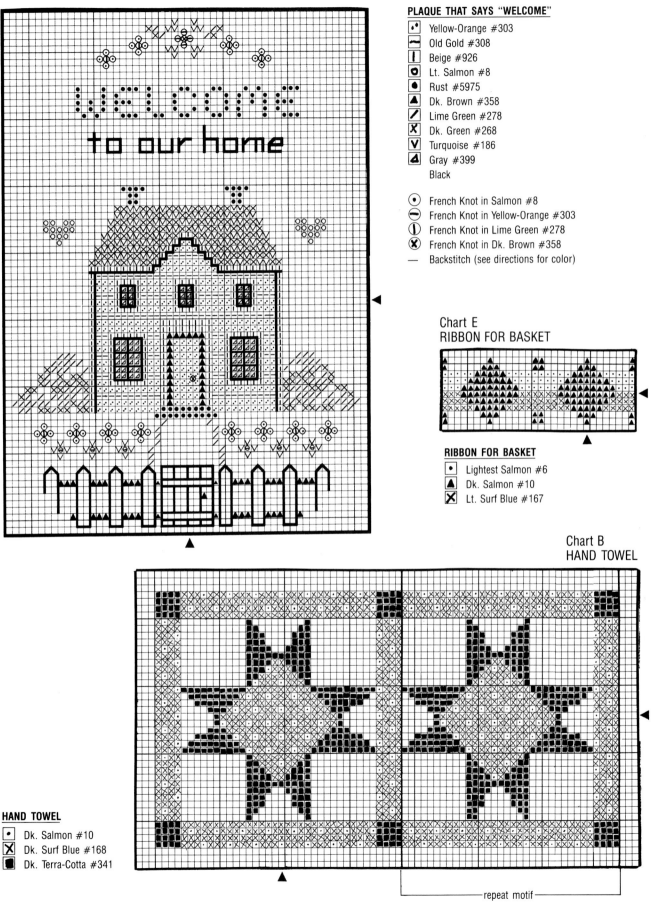

PLAQUE THAT SAYS "WELCOME"

- Yellow-Orange #303
- Old Gold #308
- Beige #926
- Lt. Salmon #8
- Rust #5975
- Dk. Brown #358
- Lime Green #278
- Dk. Green #268
- Turquoise #186
- Gray #399
- Black

- ⊙ French Knot in Salmon #8
- ⊖ French Knot in Yellow-Orange #303
- Ⓘ French Knot in Lime Green #278
- Ⓧ French Knot in Dk. Brown #358
- — Backstitch (see directions for color)

Chart E
RIBBON FOR BASKET

RIBBON FOR BASKET

- • Lightest Salmon #6
- ▲ Dk. Salmon #10
- ✗ Lt. Surf Blue #167

Chart B
HAND TOWEL

HAND TOWEL

- • Dk. Salmon #10
- ✗ Dk. Surf Blue #168
- ▮ Dk. Terra-Cotta #341

repeat motif

25

A Sign for Condo Dwellers

This little kitty is here to say that your home can still have a country look even if you live in the city. Seated on a braided rug, the domestic tabby extols the virtues of condominium living. The picture is worked with floss on an even-weave fabric.

SIZE: Design area, 5¼″ × 7¾″.

EQUIPMENT: Ruler. Iron. Tapestry needle. Frame and mat.

MATERIALS: Ecru Aida cloth (18-count), piece at least 8″ × 10″. DMC 6-strand embroidery floss, one 8-meter skein of each color listed in color key.

DIRECTIONS: See "Cross-Stitch Basics," page 74. Prepare Aida as directed, basting to mark center point. From center point, measure ½″ to the left and 2½″ up for first stitch. With 2 strands of floss in tapestry needle, work design in cross-stitch by fol-

lowing chart and color key and beginning with light golden-brown stitch at arrow; make cross-stitches in face area as charted.

When cross-stitch has been completed, work backstitching with 1 strand of floss, following solid lines on chart: With medium brown, outline pink nose, muzzle, and mouth. With dark brown, define sides of nose, inner ears, and toes and outline body. With dark blue, outline and define bow. With 1 strand of white floss, straight-stitch whiskers.

FINISHING: Press piece facedown on well-padded surface. Mat and frame as desired.

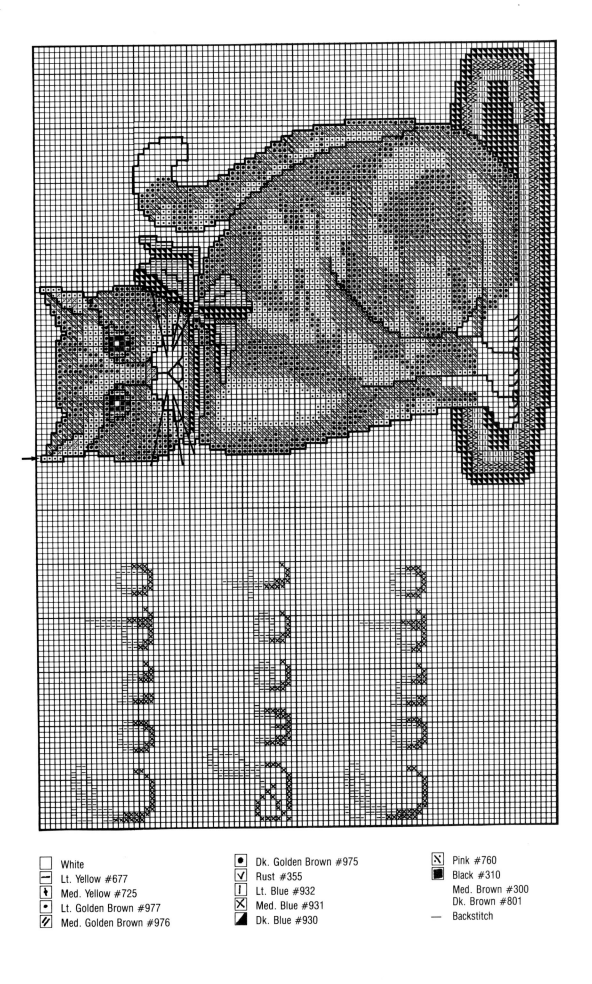

	White		Dk. Golden Brown #975		Pink #760
	Lt. Yellow #677		Rust #355		Black #310
	Med. Yellow #725		Lt. Blue #932		Med. Brown #300
	Lt. Golden Brown #977		Med. Blue #931		Dk. Brown #801
	Med. Golden Brown #976		Dk. Blue #930		— Backstitch

Patchwork Pillows from the Past

Combine quilting and cross-stitching techniques to make these calico pillows. First stitch pastel folk-art motifs or crewel-inspired blue and white flowers onto the center panels; then surround the cross-stitched squares with the colorful machine-pieced borders. Double ruffles add the finishing touches.

BLUE RUFFLED PILLOWS

SIZE: 16″ square, plus 2½″ ruffle.

EQUIPMENT: Masking tape. Iron. Straight pins. Embroidery hoop. Embroidery needles. Scissors. Ruler. Pencil with eraser. Cardboard. T or carpenter's square or graph paper. Dressmaker's marking pencils in light and dark colors. Sewing machine.

MATERIALS: **For each pillow:** Ivory Aida cloth (14-count), one 8″ square. DMC 6-strand embroidery floss, 1 skein of each color listed in color key. Cotton fabrics 44″ wide: ivory with blue print, medium blue print, navy print, and solid navy. **For Pillow A,** ½ yard each of ivory print, blue print, solid navy, and small amounts of navy print. **For Pillow B,** ½ yard solid navy and navy print, small amounts of ivory and blue prints. Blue sewing thread. Fiberfill or pillow form, 16″ square.

DIRECTIONS: Prewash all fabrics to preshrink; let dry, then press.

Cross-Stitching: See "Cross-Stitch Basics," page 74. Prepare Aida fabric as directed. Fold in half in both directions to find exact center; count 2 "squares" of fabric threads to the right and mark fabric square with pin. Place fabric in hoop. Work either design in cross-stitch, following color key and chart for Pillow A or Pillow B. Begin at pin with stitch indicated by arrows. For each cross-stitch, use 2 strands of floss in needle and work over 1 "square" of fabric threads. For Pillow B, add backstitches using 1 strand of dark blue floss and following heavy lines on chart for position of stitches.

When embroidery has been completed, remove fabric from hoop and tape from fabric edges; press. With design centered, trim edges of fabric evenly to make a 6¼″ square (this includes ⅜″ seam allowances all around).

Cutting Pillow Pieces: From navy fabric, cut a 17″ square; set aside for pillow back. From 2 contrasting fabrics (see color photograph), cut strips on the bias and piece for a total length of 128″; cut one 5¾″ wide and the other 4¼″ wide; set aside for ruffles.

Pillow Top Pattern: On a large sheet of paper, use pencil and ruler to mark a 16″ square. Use either a T or carpenter's square, or work on graph paper to ensure right corners. Divide 16″ square in half horizontally and vertically to form 4 quarters, then further divide each quarter into quarters. You should now have sixteen 4″ squares (see Figure 1). Following either Figure 2 for Pillow A or Figure 3 for Pillow B, divide each 4″ square in half diagonally. Shade resulting triangles as shown, or label with matching letters (for example, A for all ivory print). Erase lines between adjacent same-shaded triangles. Cut out 1 of each different shape, glue to cardboard, let dry, then cut out for templates.

Following appropriate diagram, use templates to mark on wrong side of designated fabric for the necessary number of pieces; place longest edge along fabric grain and ⅜″ from fabric edges, leaving at least ¾″ between pieces. Using dressmaker's marking pencil, trace around template. Trace around again ⅜″ beyond outline for seam allowances, then cut out piece along outer marked line. Arrange pieces as shown in diagram.

Piecing: To stitch pieces together, pin right sides facing, with matching raw edges even. Stitch along inner marked line, making a ⅜″ seam. Begin by stitching a blue print triangle to each side of Aida cloth square. Within each row, stitch triangles together to form squares or rectangles. Stitch squares and rectangles together within each row. Finally, stitch rows together, taking care to match seams.

ASSEMBLY: To make ruffles, stitch ends of each bias strip together to form a ring. Press each strip in half lengthwise, wrong sides facing. Place narrower strip on top of wider strip, with raw edges even. Run a gathering thread through all layers ¼″ from raw edges and pull up thread to gather ring to half its circumference. Pin around pillow front, distributing gathers generously at the corners and evenly along each side. Baste ⅜″ from raw edges. Pin on top of pillow back. Stitch along basting stitches all around, leaving opening along one side. Insert pillow form or stuff with fiberfill until plump. Turn open edges to inside and slip-stitch closed.

PINK PATCHWORK PILLOWS

SIZES: 12″–13″ square, with 2¾″ double ruffle all around.

EQUIPMENT: Straight pins. Ruler. Pencil or dressmaker's marking pencil. Iron. Scissors. Cardboard. Sewing machine.

MATERIALS: For all: Davosa cotton fabric (18-count) by Zweigart (see Source Guide, page 78), 12″ squares, 2 pink #430, 1 blue #507. DMC pearl cotton #5: 2 skeins of each color listed in color key. Cotton fabrics 44″ wide: muslin, 1½ yards; calicoes: 1⅛ yards each of berry mini-print, pink, and blue; ⅜ yard each of white/pink, white/blue, light blue dot, light blue floral; ⅛ yard of berry floral. Pink sewing thread. White carpet or quilting thread. Fiberfill.

DIRECTIONS: Cross-Stitch Embroidery: See "Cross-Stitch Basics," page 74. Prepare Davosa fabric as directed. Fold Davosa fabric in quarters to locate center; mark fabric thread with a pin. Work fabric in cross-stitch, following color key and charts for Pillow 1 (pink Davosa), 2 (blue Davosa), or 3 (pink Davosa). To begin, work first cross-stitch (indicated by arrows on chart) at pin mark. Work each cross-stitch over 1 "square" of 2 horizontal and 2 vertical threads; use 1 strand of pearl cotton in needle. Chart for Pillow 3 shows left half of design only. Follow chart, then repeat in reverse, omitting center row, to work right half of design.

Pillow Tops: All measurements include ¼″ seam allowances unless otherwise indicated. Using pencil or dressmaker's marking pencil, mark pieces on wrong side of fabrics with longest edges along the grain. Pin pieces together, with right sides facing and matching edges even; make ¼″ seams. Press seam allowances toward the darker fabric as you go.

PILLOW 1

Measure a 7″ square around embroidery. Draw out 1 thread on each side of square to mark stitching line, then cut out ¼″ beyond drawn threads. Make a cardboard template for a 1½″-square patch. Place template on wrong side of fabric and trace around lightly with pencil. Cut out ¼″ beyond marked line for seam allowance. In this manner, cut 28 patches from white/pink fabric and 29 patches from light blue dot fabric. Arrange, checkerboard fashion, into strips 2 patches wide: two 5 patches long and two 9 patches long. Join each strip: Stitch patches into rows, then stitch rows together. Stitch short strips to sides of embroidery, then stitch long strips to top and bottom. Pillow top should measure 13½″ square.

PILLOW 2

Measure a 7″ square around embroidery. Draw out 1 thread on each side of square to mark stitching line, then cut out ¼″ beyond drawn threads. Cut out 1½″-wide strips to the following lengths: from pink calico, 7½″ (A), 8½″ (C), 12½″ (J), and 13½″ (L); from berry mini-print, 8½″ (B) and 9½″ (D); from light blue print, 9½″ (E) and 10½″ (G); from white/blue print, 10½″ (F) and 11½″ (H); from berry floral, 11½″ (I) and 12½″ (K). Stitch strips around embroidery log-cabin style: Pin A along one side of embroidery; stitch and press. Working clockwise and matching joined edges with new strip, join B along an adjacent side of embroidery. Join C along third side and D along fourth side. You should now have a 9½″ square. Working in same manner, enlarge the square with strips E, F, G, and H. Repeat with I, J, K, and L. Pillow top should measure 13½″ square, including seam allowances.

PILLOW 3

Measure an 8″ square around embroidery. Draw out 1 thread on each side of square to mark stitching line, then cut out ¼″ beyond drawn threads. Cut strips 1½″ × 8½″: 4 each from light blue dot fabric and pink calico. Pin strips together in unmatched pairs and stitch along one long edge. With blue strips on the inside, stitch a strip-pair to top and bottom of embroidery. Cut 1½″ squares: 8 each from blue calico and berry floral. Arrange 2 blue and 2 berry squares into 2 rows of 2, with same-color patches catty-corner to each other. Stitch into rows, then stitch rows together to form a 2½″-square unit, including seam allowances. Repeat with remaining square patches for a total of 4 square units. Stitch to either side of two remaining strip-pairs so light blue dot strip is adjacent to blue calico patch. Stitch to sides of embroidery, placing light blue dot strips on the inside, centering carefully, and taking care to match seams. Pillow top should measure 12½″ square, including seam allowances.

PILLOW ASSEMBLY: Cut squares ¼″ larger all around than pillow top: 1 from a calico fabric for backing and 2 from muslin for lining. Baste muslin square (centering carefully) to wrong sides of pillow top and backing.

Cutting across entire width of fabric, cut two 6¼″-wide strips from same fabric as backing, and two 4¾″-wide strips from a different fabric for front ruffle (refer to color photograph for fabric suggestions). Stitch matching strips together at one short end, then stitch free ends together to form a ring. Fold each ruffle in half lengthwise, wrong sides together; press. Place front ruffle over back ruffle, matching raw edges. Place carpet or quilting thread ¼″ from raw edges and zigzag-stitch over it. Pull carpet thread to gather ruffles to fit around pillow top. Pin around pillow top, even with muslin, distributing gathers generously at corners and evenly along sides. Baste ⅜″ from edge. Place on top of backing, right sides facing, and stitch all around along basting line, leaving a 5″ opening at center of one side. Stuff pillow plumply, then turn raw edges to inside and slip-stitch closed.

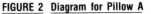

FABRIC KEY

☐	Aida Cloth
⦂	Ivory Print
⦿	Blue Print
⦂	Navy Print
▦	Navy Solid

FIGURE 1 16″

16″

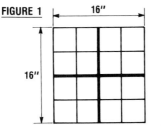

FIGURE 2 Diagram for Pillow A

Row 1

Row 2

Row 3

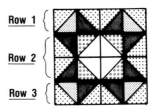

FIGURE 3 Diagram for Pillow B

Row 1

Row 2

Row 3

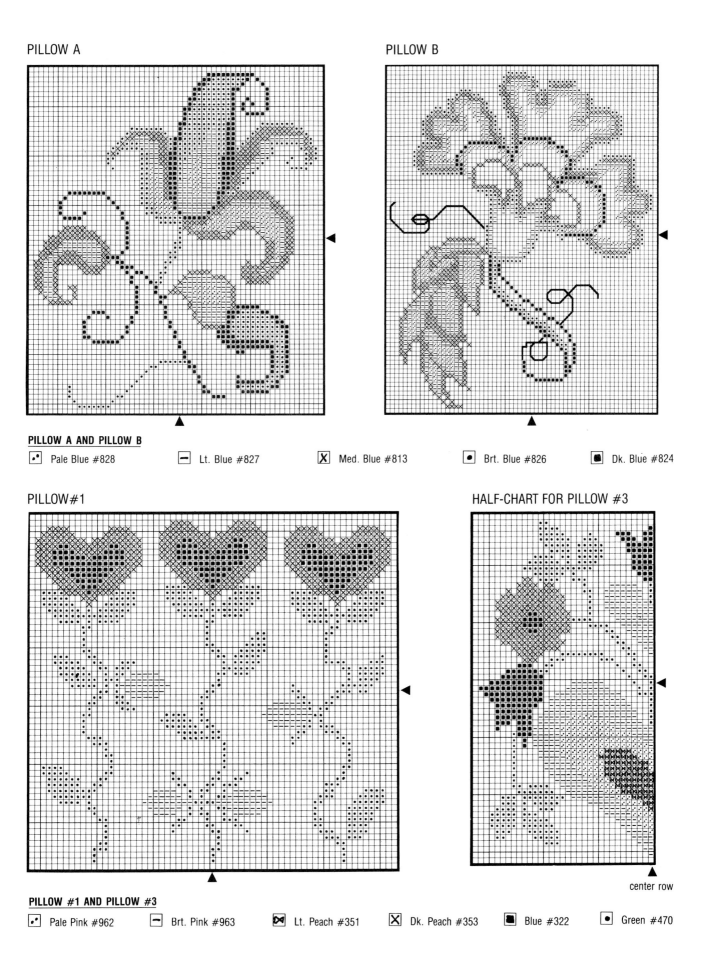

PILLOW A

PILLOW B

PILLOW A AND PILLOW B

`•` Pale Blue #828   `−` Lt. Blue #827   `X` Med. Blue #813   `•` Brt. Blue #826   `■` Dk. Blue #824

PILLOW#1

HALF-CHART FOR PILLOW #3

center row

PILLOW #1 AND PILLOW #3

`•` Pale Pink #962   `−` Brt. Pink #963   `⋈` Lt. Peach #351   `X` Dk. Peach #353   `■` Blue #322   `•` Green #470

PILLOW #2

PILLOW #2

∴	Pale Pink #962
—	Brt. Pink #963
⋈	Lt. Peach #351
■	Blue #322
•	Green #470

Monogrammed Motifs

Although this graceful alphabet can be cross-stitched onto just about anything, we've chosen to duplicate it on crisp white bed linens and pillows. The elegant letters with the delicate leaf-and-berry designs will lend a personal touch to your accessories.

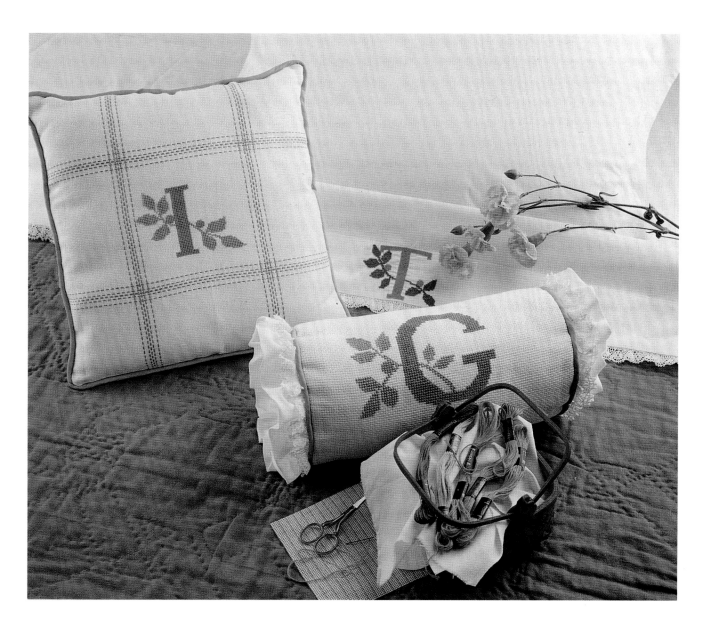

EQUIPMENT: Straight pins. Embroidery needles. Pencil. Sewing machine with zipper foot. Scissors.

MATERIALS: DMC 6-strand embroidery floss, 1 skein each of blue, light green or kelly green, and pink. See individual project directions for additional materials.

GENERAL DIRECTIONS: See "Cross-Stitch Basics," page 74. For pillows, prepare fabric edges as directed. Fold fabric into quarters to locate center; mark with a pin. Work chart in cross-stitch, using number of strands of floss indicated in directions for individual items. Refer to photograph for our color suggestions; follow black-and-white charts for easier readability. On black-and-white charts, arrows indicate center of letter, not entire design. Individual directions suggest that you center either letter or entire design. To center entire design, count squares on chart to locate center row horizontally and vertically. Point at which rows converge indicates center of entire design; mark with a pencil. Begin at pin mark either with stitch indicated on chart by arrows (to center letter) or with stitch indicated by your pencil mark (to center entire design). If there is no symbol in that square, count to the nearest symbol, then count threads on fabric to correspond and start there. Work letter in blue, berries in pink, stems and leaves in light or kelly green as desired.

PILLOW

SIZE: 13″ square.

ADDITIONAL MATERIALS: Shenandoah fabric from Zweigart, one 15″ square with blue grid centered. White medium-weight cotton for lining and pillow back, three 15″ squares. Blue cording ¼″ thick, 1½ yards. White sewing thread. Fiberfill.

DIRECTIONS: Work desired monogram in center of even-weave fabric, following General Directions above and centering entire design. Work each cross-stitch over 1 "square" of 2 horizontal and 2 vertical fabric threads, using 2 strands of floss in needle.

Pin and baste linings to back of pillow front and back. Pin, then machine-baste cording around pillow front; use a zipper foot to get as close as possible to cording. Place front on pillow back, right sides facing. Sew along basting stitches, leaving opening along center of bottom. Clip corners, turn to right side, and stuff plumply with fiberfill. Turn open edges to inside and slip-stitch closed.

BOLSTER

SIZE: 11″ long, plus ruffle.

SPECIAL EQUIPMENT: Compass.

ADDITIONAL MATERIALS: White Aida cloth (11-count), 12″ × 18″ piece. White cotton fabric 44″ wide, ½ yard. White lace trim 1¼″ wide, 1 yard. Blue cording ¼″ thick, 1 yard. White sewing thread. Fiberfill.

DIRECTIONS: Hold Aida cloth with short edges at top and bottom. Cross-stitch desired monogram in center, centering letter. Using 3 strands of floss in needle, work each cross-stitch over 1 "square" of 1 horizontal and 1 vertical group of fabric threads.

From white fabric, cut one 12″ × 18″ rectangle for lining, two 6″ circles for sides, and two 4″ × 36″ strips on the bias for ruffles. Baste lining to back of embroidery. Make ruffles: Seam ends of each strip together, forming a ring. With wrong sides facing, fold strip in half lengthwise; press. Baste ¼″ from raw edges and draw up threads to gather to half strip's length. Pin a ruffle around each circle. Baste ¼″ from edges. With right sides facing and edges even, pin cording (with white lace trim on top) to long edges of embroidery. Machine-baste through all 3 layers, using a zipper foot to get as close as possible to cording. With right sides facing, pin each long edge of embroidery fabric around a circle; hand-stitch along previous stitching lines through all layers. Clip edges of circles and turn bolster to right side. Stuff with fiberfill, turn short edges to inside, and slip-stitch closed.

TOP SHEET

SIZE: As desired.

ADDITIONAL MATERIALS: Purchased white flat bed sheet. Waste canvas (16-count), 4″ × 6″ rectangle. White lace trim ⅞″ wide, long enough to trim top edge of sheet. Masking tape. White sewing thread.

DIRECTIONS: Vanishing or "waste" canvas is a lightweight mesh used as a guide for working cross-stitches on fabrics where threads cannot be counted. To prevent raveling, bind raw edges of waste canvas with masking tape. Locate and mark center of wide hem at top of sheet. Pin waste canvas centered on top. Be sure to work letter on wrong side of sheet facing edge; when sheet is turned back letter will be right side up. Work following appropriate chart; center letter and use 2 strands of floss in needle.

When embroidery has been completed, carefully draw out waste canvas threads, one at a time. Draw out 1 horizontal, then 1 vertical thread, and so on, until the canvas has "vanished" or "wasted" away, leaving finished cross-stitch design in fabric. Machine-stitch bound or raw edge of lace under edge of hem.

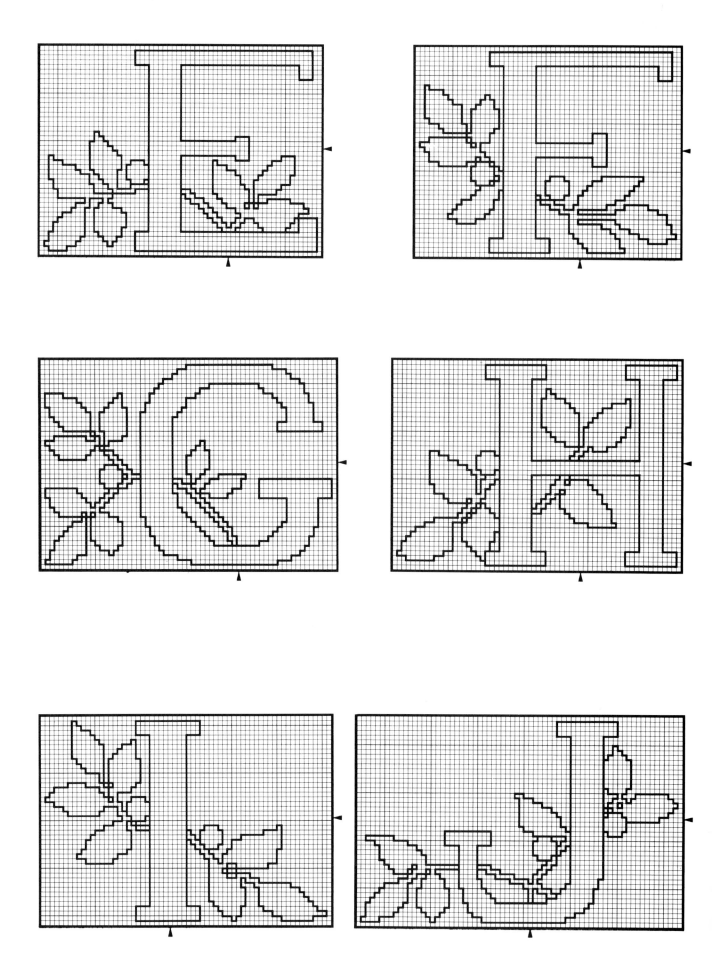

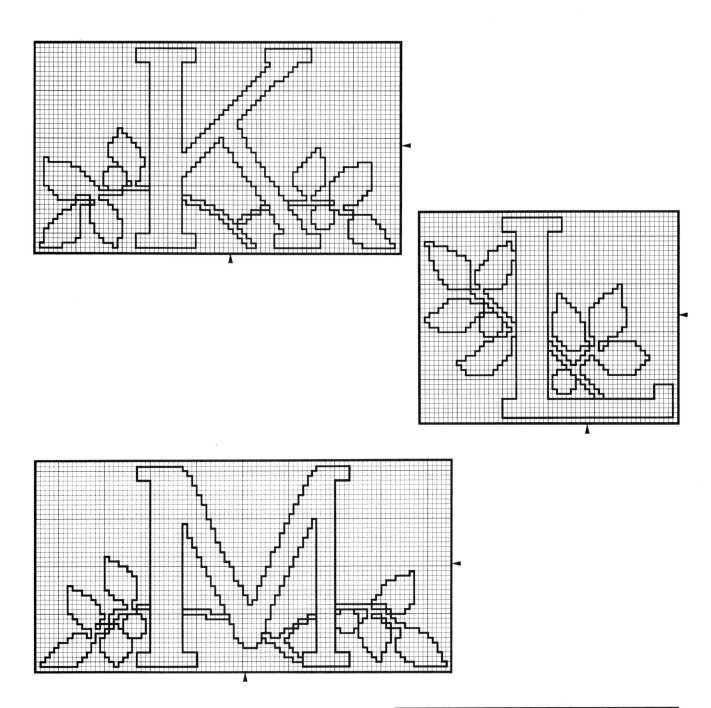

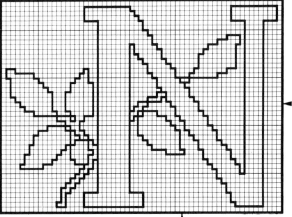

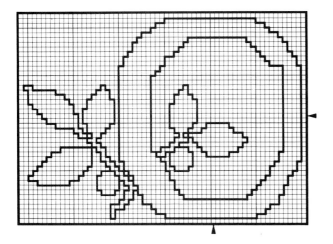

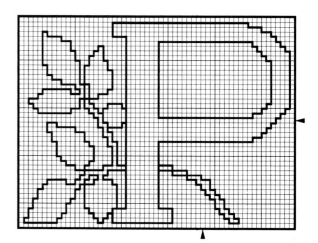

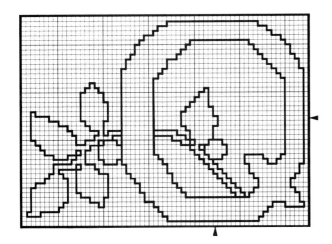

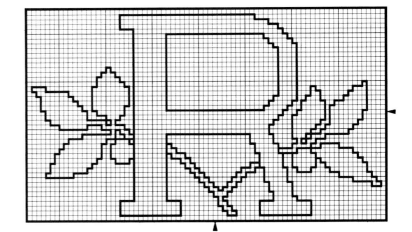

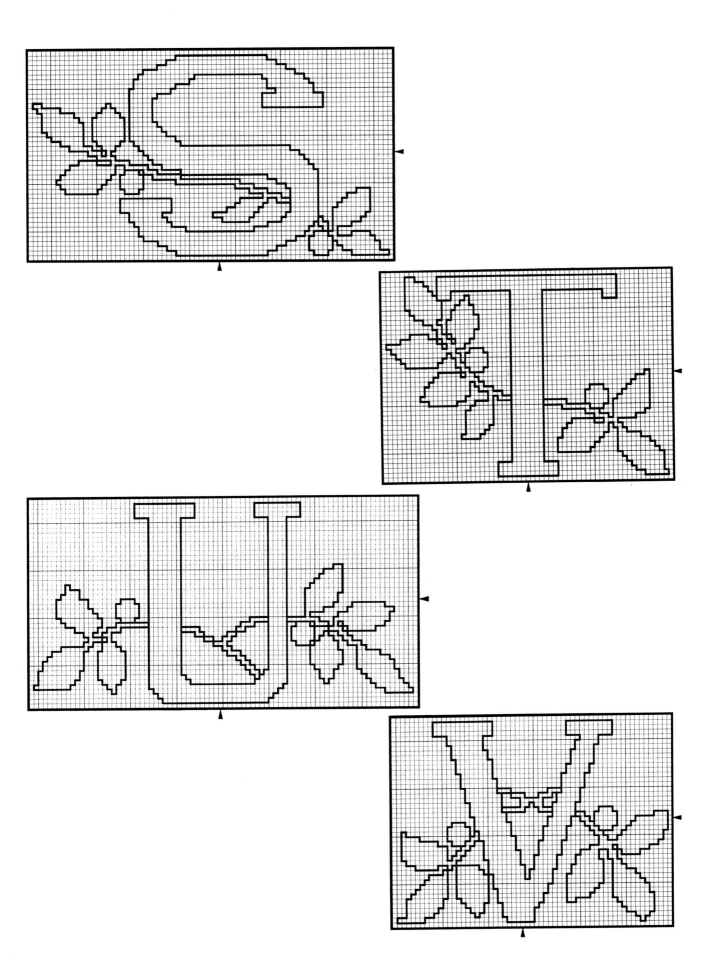

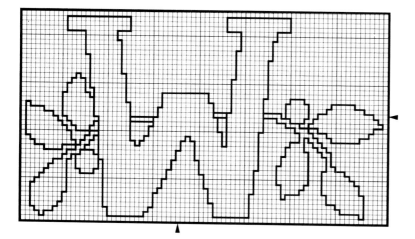

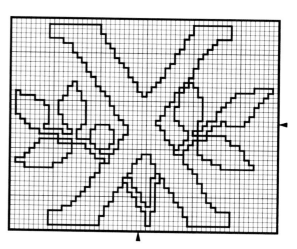

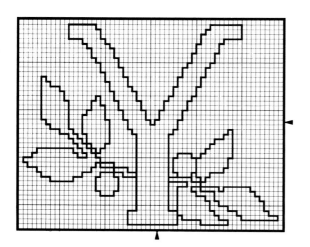

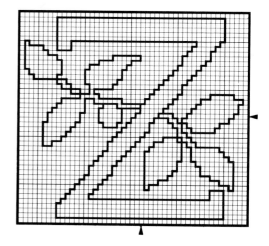

TRADITIONAL TREASURES

Certain crafts are just meant to be passed down from generation to generation, as is the case with these old-fashioned collectibles. All the objects in this series embody an antique quality and have their roots in designs from the past. Because folk art has become so popular, two kinds have been included—American and European—to capture the multifaceted flavor of this unique handiwork. Why not stitch up one of these nostalgic treasures that will be valued for years to come?

A Sampler Etched in History

This sampler is based on a design that was originally stitched in 1849 by a little girl named Mary Ann Fowler. The stylized floral border, numbers, block alphabet, and pious sentiment are typical of samplers from that era.

SIZE: 16½" × 17¼".

EQUIPMENT: Graph paper. Sewing thread and sewing needles. Colored pencil. Embroidery needles.

MATERIALS: Beige Hardanger fabric (22-count), one 21½" × 23" piece. DMC 6-strand embroidery floss, one 8-meter skein of each color in color key unless otherwise indicated in parentheses.

DIRECTIONS: See "Cross-Stitch Basics," page 74. Prepare fabric as directed.

Guidelines: Using contrasting thread, baste a center line from top to bottom and from side to side by following a row of threads.

Using sharp colored pencil and following arrows on chart, draw center lines to correspond with basting on fabric.

For Main Chart: Each square on chart represents 2 fabric threads. Work cross-stitches over 2 fabric threads in each direction, using 2 strands of floss in needle. Begin at exact center on fabric at stitch indicated on chart by arrows.

For Motto and Name Block: Each square on chart represents 1 fabric thread. Work cross-stitches over 1 thread in each direction, using 1 strand of dark brown floss in needle. Work capital G as for L and H, using 2 strands over 2 fabric threads as indicated. Center name block between baskets 4 fabric threads below wreath.

●	Dk. Green (2) #520
─	Med. Green (2) #3363
╱	Pale Green #523
○	Mint Green #504
◢	Dk. Brown #938
V	Med. Brown #434
╲	Spice #922
⊼	Crimson #816
✕	Red (2) #321
Ⅰ	Salmon #760
•	Pale Peach #225
▼	Colonial Blue #930
✝	Aqua #598
∴	Beige #738
S	Soft Yellow #744

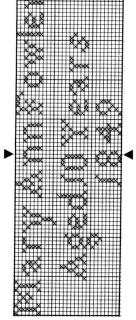

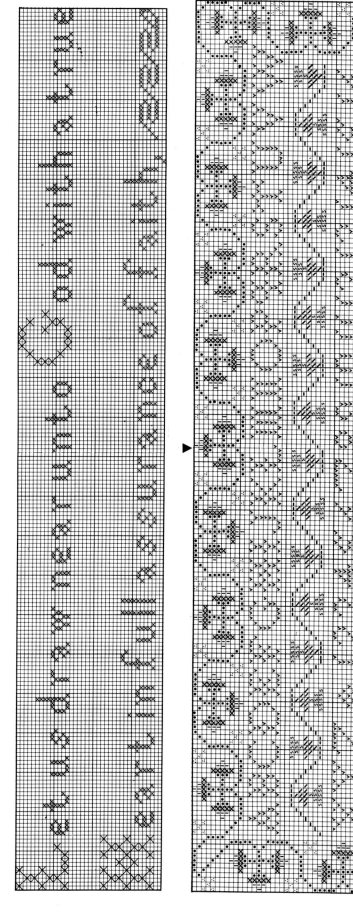

Old World Stitchery

The patterns shown here represent a type of folk art that is based in Eastern European cultures. The dark blue background sets off the gaily colored stitchery, which will add Continental charm to pillows, curtains, and other decorative items.

EQUIPMENT: Scissors. Pencil. Masking tape. Sewing thread and sewing needles. Embroidery needle. Iron.

MATERIALS: Navy Aida cloth (14-count); see individual directions for amounts. DMC 6-strand embroidery floss, one 8-meter skein of each color listed in color key. For additional materials, see directions for individual items.

GENERAL DIRECTIONS: See "Cross-Stitch Basics," page 74. Cut or mark fabric as specified in directions for individual items. Prepare cut fabric edges for embroidery with masking tape. Baste along center threads both horizontally and vertically. Use 3 strands of floss in needle and work over 1 "square" of horizontal and vertical fabric threads. Charts show upper right quarter or right half of the design. Arrows indicate center rows; the

square common to center column and row is center stitch. Begin at center of fabric with center stitch. If there is no symbol at exact center, count chart squares to the nearest symbol and count fabric threads to correspond.

For quarter charts, start at center and stitch upper right quarter of fabric. Turn chart counterclockwise a quarter turn to work upper left quarter; omit vertical center row. Be sure all cross-stitches overlap in same direction as before. Turn chart in same manner to work lower left quarter; omit horizontal center row. Turn chart again and work remaining (lower right) quarter, omitting both center rows.

For half charts, follow chart to work right half, stitching to the right of the vertical basting thread. Work left half by following directions for individual items.

Remove basting stitches. Press completed embroidery on a well-padded surface. Mount and frame pieces as indicated below.

TRAY

SIZE: 17″ square; design area, 8½″ × 9½″.

ADDITIONAL MATERIALS: Aida cloth, 12″ square. Square colonial tray #320-P in antique red from Sunshine Station (see Source Guide, page 78). Masonite board. Pink mat board. Fabric glue.

DIRECTIONS: Work cross-stitches on Aida cloth by following Chart A, which is a quarter chart. Trim fabric to ¼″ from outer row of stitching all around. Center carefully on masonite board and glue fabric edges to secure. Have mat board cut to same size as masonite, with a centered window opening bevel-cut to ⅝″ beyond stitching all around. Place mat and glass on top of masonite and insert in tray.

PICTURE

SIZE: Framed, 15⅜″ × 14⅝″; design area, 8⅞″ × 9¾″.

ADDITIONAL MATERIALS: Aida cloth, 18″ square. Heavy cardboard. Frame, painted antique red (optional), dimensions as given above. Pale pink mat board. Glass or Plexiglas cut to fit frame opening.

DIRECTIONS: Work cross-stitches on right half of Aida cloth by following Chart B, which is a half chart. Turn chart upside down and follow to work left half of fabric, omitting vertical center row.

Mount needlework over heavy cardboard cut to fit inside frame, centering carefully. Have a beveled mat cut to fit within rabbet of frame, with a centered window opening ⅜″ larger all around than cross-stitched border. Insert mat, mounted embroidery, and optional glass or Plexiglas into frame.

PILLOW

SIZE: 11″ × 10½″.

ADDITIONAL MATERIALS: Aida cloth, 13″ × 12½″. Same-size piece of bright pink cotton fabric for pillow back. Bright pink passementerie or soutache braid ⅜″ wide, 1½ yards. Pink thread. Clear nylon sewing thread. Fiberfill.

DIRECTIONS: Cross-stitch Aida cloth by following Chart C, which is a quarter chart. Trim fabric to 1″ beyond stitching. Trim pink fabric to same size for pillow back. With right sides facing, place pillow front and back together and stitch around, ⅜″ beyond stitching, leaving a 5″ opening at center of one side. Clip away seam allowance across corners; turn to right side. Stuff plumply with fiberfill; turn raw edges to inside and slip-stitch closed. Starting at a corner, use pink thread to slip-stitch braid around pillow, centering it over seam and stitching along both long edges. At each corner, use 2″ of braid to make a loop. If desired, use nylon thread to whipstitch over braid, pulling stitches taut to roll braid and simulate a corded edge.

HAND MIRROR

SIZE: 12″ long; design area, 5″ in diameter.

ADDITIONAL MATERIALS: Aida cloth, 7″ square. White enamel Needlework Hand Mirror from Sudberry House. (See Source Guide, page 78.) Small amount of batting or fiberfill. Bright pink scalloped (crocheted) lace trim ½″ wide, ½ yard. Fabric glue.

DIRECTIONS: Cross-stitch right half of fabric by following Chart D, which is a half pattern. For left half, work chart in reverse but omit vertical center row. Glue a small amount of batting or fiberfill to the mounting board, then follow manufacturer's instructions for mounting cross-stitched fabric. Glue lace trim to back of mounting board all around, letting ¼″ extend past edges. Glue covered board to back of mirror.

HEART SACHET

SIZE: 5½″.

ADDITIONAL MATERIALS: Aida cloth, 7″ square. Same-size square of bright pink cotton fabric for backing. Pink thread. Bright pink scalloped (crocheted) lace trim ½″ wide, ½ yard. Fiberfill. Potpourri, 1 tablespoon.

DIRECTIONS: Cross-stitch right half of Aida cloth by following Chart E, which is a half chart. For left half, work chart in reverse but omit vertical center row. Trim fabric to 1″ beyond stitching; cut bright pink fabric to same shape for sachet back. With right sides facing, place cross-stitched front on back. Stitch around, making a ½″ seam and leaving 3″ along one side unstitched. Clip into seam allowance along curves and angles; turn sachet to right side. Stuff partway, make a small well at center, and pour in potpourri. Finish stuffing. Turn open edges to inside and slip-stitch closed. Starting and ending at top center, slip-stitch straight edge of lace trim around pillow along seam; overlap ends neatly.

Chart A
TRAY

Chart D
HAND MIRROR

Chart C
PILLOW

••	Pale Pink #963
I	Med. Pink #962
+	Brt. Pink #602
X	Red #666
△	Lime Green #704
▲	Kelly Green #703
—	Lt. Blue #813
■	Purple #553

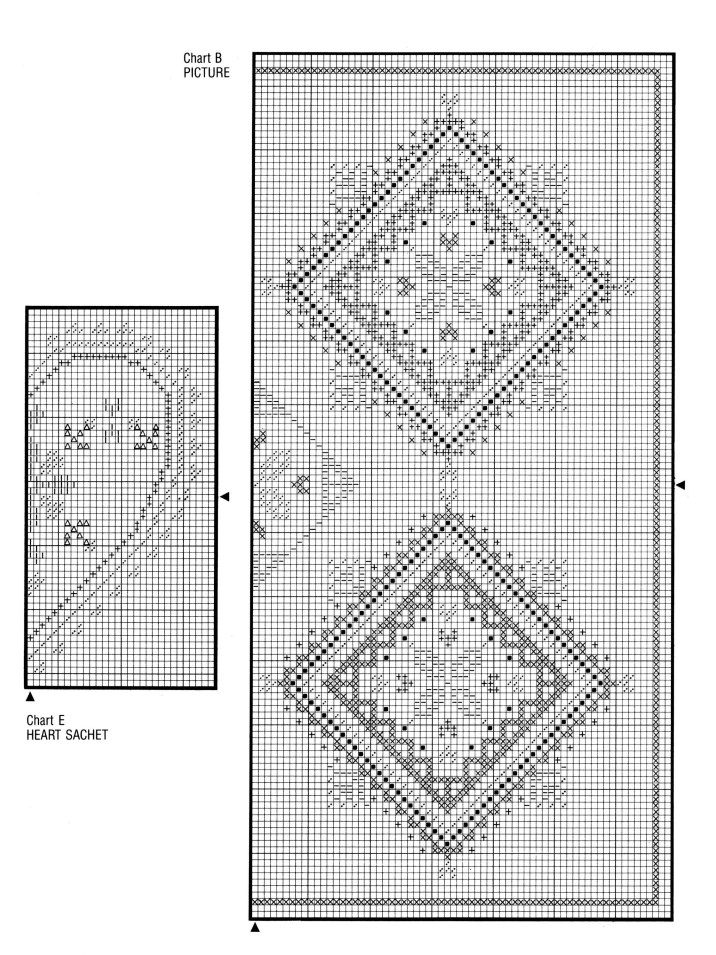

Chart E
HEART SACHET

Kittens and Flowers Alphabet Sampler

Here's a sampler that has both conventional and modern elements. A simple carnation border frames the traditional flower-sprinkled alphabet, while an elegant vase of tulips and a pair of stately Siamese cats lend a contemporary touch.

SIZE: 15″ × 18″ within mat.

EQUIPMENT: Sewing thread and needle. Red pencil. Embroidery hoop. Embroidery needles. Iron.

MATERIALS: Peach linen fabric (25-count), 55″ wide, piece 18″ × 24″. Susan Bates/Anchor embroidery floss, 1 skein of each color listed in color key unless otherwise indicated in parentheses. Mat and frame as desired.

DIRECTIONS: See "Cross-Stitch Basics," page 74. Prepare fabric as directed. Fold fabric into quarters. Using sewing thread of a contrasting color, baste along center of fabric both horizontally and vertically. Using red pencil, draw along grid lines on chart indicated by arrows.

Place center of fabric in hoop. Stitch design, working cross-stitches first, then backstitches, by following chart and color key. Work with 2 strands of floss throughout, and work each stitch over a "square" of 2 horizontal and 2 vertical fabric threads. Begin at center of fabric with light citrus stitch at intersection of red lines drawn on chart.

When all embroidery has been completed, remove fabric from hoop and remove basting threads. Press and mount as described in "Cross-Stich Basics"; mat and frame as desired.

Symbol	Color		Symbol	Color		Symbol	Color		Symbol	Color	BACKSTITCH

Λ   Snow White #1
·   Very Lt. Salmon #6 (3)
−   Lt. Salmon #8 (3)
X   Med. Salmon #9 (3)

■   Dk. Salmon #11
\   Lt. Sapphire #159
/   Lt. Sea Green #185

+   Med. Sea Green #186 (3)
●   Dk. Sea Green #187 (3)
| Lt. Citrus #301
:   Lt. Flesh #778

V   Med. Flesh #868
▲   Larkspur #929

BACKSTITCH
___ Dk. Carnation #29 (3)
___ Dk. Sea Green #187
___ Larkspur #929
---- Brick #5975

FLORAL FANTASIES

Lovely flowers bloom on this crop of projects, bringing the pleasures of the garden indoors to be enjoyed all year long. Botanical delights, such as vine-ripened fruits, springtime bouquets, and romantic roses grace pillow, sampler, and picture designs, and even show up on some old-fashioned notecards. Keep these crafts in mind for all your green-thumb friends.

Bunnies and Bouquets

What could be more charming than a bouquet of roses or a blossom-covered bunny set within lacey borders? Cross-stitched in springtime pastels, these designs are perfect for pictures or pillows.

BUNNY PICTURE AND ROSE BOUQUET PILLOW

⦂	White
−	Gray #762
I	Pale Pink #819
▢	Lt. Pink #3689
⊙	Med. Pink #3688
X	Deep Pink #3687
▪	Ruby #3685
O	Lilac #554
●	Purple #553
/	Pale Yellow #746
⊓	Med. Yellow #727
C	Gold #834
◥	Dk. Blue #824
▲	Brt. Blue #826
S	Lt. Green #907
V	Med. Green #988
▲	Dk. Green #986

SIZES: Picture (framed), 11″×14″; pillow, 10″ square.

EQUIPMENT: Straight pins. Embroidery needle. Iron. Scissors.

MATERIALS: For both: Aida cloth (14-count), one 15″×20″ pink rectangle for picture; one 12″ light blue square for pillow. DMC 6-strand embroidery floss: 9 skeins white, 1 skein of every other color listed in color key. **For picture:** Mat board 11″×14″. Frame to fit. **For pillow:** Pink cotton fabric, 11″ square. White sewing thread. White soutache braid or lace trim with one scalloped edge ⅜″ wide, 1¼ yards. Fiberfill.

DIRECTIONS: See "Cross-Stitch Basics," page 74. Prepare Aida fabric as directed. Fold fabric in quarters to locate center; mark fabric thread with a pin. Work on pink Aida by following chart for picture or on blue Aida by following chart for pillow. To begin, work first cross-stitch (indicated by arrows on chart) at pin mark. Work each cross-stitch over a "square" of 1 horizontal and 1 vertical thread group. Use 3 strands of floss in needle for cross-stitches. A quarter of border is shown. Work

upper right quarter as shown. Work border in reverse to complete upper left quarter, then work top half in reverse to complete lower half of border. For Bunny Picture, fill background within border with rows of white cross-stitches, working in the established pattern. For Rose Bouquet Pillow, work stems in long, straight stitches using 2 strands of dark green floss and following chart. On either design, when all cross-stitching has been completed, work backstitches using 1 strand of ruby floss; work each backstitch over 1 square of fabric threads.

FINISHING: Picture: Finish and mount, following directions in "Cross-Stitch Basics." **Pillow:** Press embroidery and trim to an 11″ square. Pin, then baste white trim around embroidery with straight edge of trim ⅜″ from edges of Aida fabric; ease trim around corners. With right sides facing, place on pink fabric square (pillow back) and sew around along basting stitches, leaving a 5″ opening at center of bottom edge. Clip corners and turn pillow to right side. Stuff pillow plumply, turn open edges to inside, and slip-stitch closed.

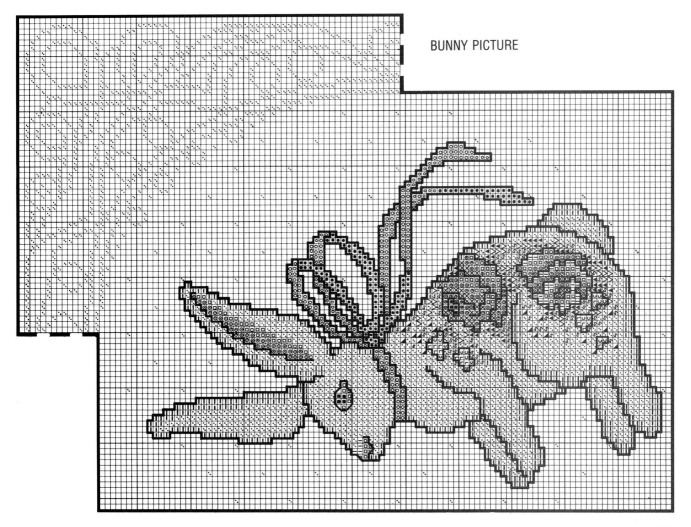

BUNNY PICTURE

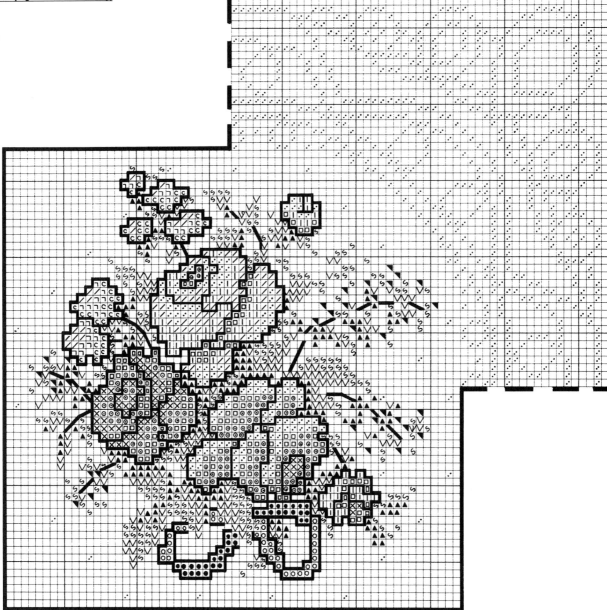

Strawberry Blossom Pillow

Out of the strawberry patch and into your home comes this country-fresh pillow. The eye-catching strawberry blossom motif is cross-stitched with floss and trimmed with polka dot and white eyelet ruffles.

SIZE: 9½" square plus ruffle.

EQUIPMENT: Ruler. Straight pins. Iron. Sewing thread. Embroidery needles.

MATERIALS: Off-white Aida cloth (14-count), 10½" square piece. Susan Bates/Anchor 6-strand embroidery floss, 1 skein each color listed in color key. Red broadcloth, 10½" square piece. Red and white polka-dot cotton fabric 36" wide, ¼ yard. Pregathered white eyelet trim 3" wide, 1½ yards. Red piping ⅜" wide, 1¼ yards. Red sewing thread. Fiberfill.

DIRECTIONS: See "Cross-Stitch Basics," page 74, and prepare Aida cloth for embroidery. From upper right corner, measure 2¼" down and 3¼" to the left; mark fabric square with pin for first stitch. Work right half of design in cross-stitch following symbols on chart and color key; use 2 strands of floss throughout. Begin at pin with stitch marked by arrow on chart. Fill in outlined berry shapes with red stitches. Work left half of pillow, reversing design and omitting tendril at bottom. When cross-stitch is completed, work yellow straight stitches for flower centers and berry seeds as indicated; for central flower, do not repeat vertical stitches.

ASSEMBLY: Press finished embroidery gently on a padded surface. Pin piping to right side of embroidery, aligning raw edges so seam will be ½" from edge of Aida; baste in place. Pin eyelet over piping, matching raw edges with Aida; baste in place. Cut a 7" × 66" ruffle strip from polka-dot fabric, piecing as necessary. Assemble pillow with ruffle (see page 77).

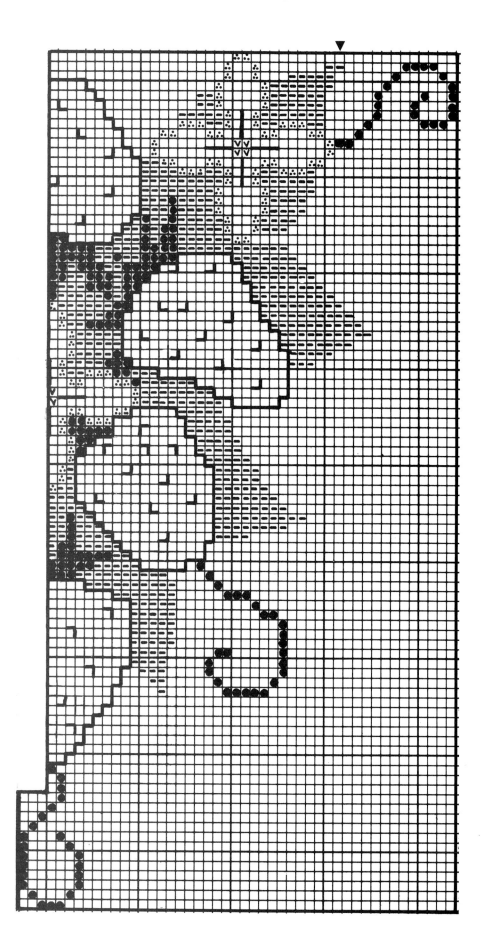

Red #46
Yellow #305
Lt. Green #254
Med. Green #255
Dk. Green #244
Straight Stitch

54

Say-It-With-Roses
Stationery and Accessories

For Mother's Day, Valentine's Day, or any time you want to send a loving message, these frilly notecards will record the sentiment in style. Stitch the roses on perforated paper, then cut, glue to fabric or stationery, and trim with ribbon, satin or lace. The designs work for bookmarks, ornaments, stationery holders, and candy-basket party favors, too.

SIZES: Bookmark, 3¼" × 7⅞" (not including loop extensions); small card, 5" × 7"; large "I love you" card, 10" × 8"; heart ornament, 5½" × 7½"; candy basket, 3½" high (not including handle); stationery holder, 8" × 10".

EQUIPMENT: Scissors. Sewing thread. Pencil with eraser. Craft glue. Embroidery needle. Straight pins. Iron.

MATERIALS: Perforated paper (14-count), one 9" × 12" sheet per project. Susan Bates/Anchor embroidery floss, colors as listed in color key: 1 skein of each per project.

See individual projects for additional materials.

GENERAL DIRECTIONS: See "Cross-Stitch Basics," page 74. Work embroidery on perforated paper by following charts for individual projects. Stitches are worked through holes on paper as for counted thread embroidery. Cut floss into 18" lengths and work with 2 strands in needle throughout. See directions for Candy Basket to plan layout of pieces on perforated paper. For all others, cut out rectangle of perforated paper with same dimensions given above for finished piece. Mark center of rectangle both horizontally and vertically with basting stitches in sewing thread of contrasting color. Begin at intersection of basting stitches with center stitch indicated on chart by arrows. If there is no symbol in that square, count to the nearest symbol, then count holes on paper to correspond. When all cross-stitch has been completed, work backstitches as indicated by chart and color key. Once all embroidery has been completed, remove basting stitches. With a pencil, mark cutting outline indicated by dotted line on chart. Cut along marked line, softening curves. Gently erase any visible pencil lines. Finish project as described below; use glue sparingly.

BOOKMARK

ADDITIONAL MATERIALS: Pink soutache braid ¼" wide, 24", or flat satin cord 1⁄16" wide, 4½ yards. Thin white paper.

FINISHING: Trim outside edges again, 3⁄16" beyond stitched outline. Place on thin paper, trace around, and cut out slightly to inside of marked line. Set aside for backing. If using satin cord, divide cord into 3 equal lengths and braid, keeping strands flat. Center lengthwise along back of card, gluing to secure. Bring ends to center back of card and glue, leaving a loop extending at top and bottom. Glue on backing.

SMALL CARD

ADDITIONAL MATERIALS: Red construction paper or tagboard.

FINISHING: From construction paper, cut a 10" × 7" rectangle. Fold in half crosswise to form a card. Glue cross-stitched paper design centered on front.

LARGE CARD

SPECIAL EQUIPMENT: Craft knife.

ADDITIONAL MATERIALS: Narrow pink satin ribbon, 1 yard. White lace trim with scalloped edge ¾" wide, ¾ yard. Red construction paper or tagboard.

FINISHING: Place cross-stitched piece on a protected surface. Using pencil, mark those areas between holes (blackened in on chart). Use craft knife to cut away these areas, creating square "eyelets" around edge. Starting and ending at bottom, weave ribbon in and out of eyelets; tie ends in a bow. From red paper, cut out a 10" × 16" rectangle. Fold in half crosswise, with fold at top, for card. Glue perforated paper heart to center of card front. Starting

and ending at center top, glue straight edge of lace trim neatly all around heart; cover edges.

HEART ORNAMENT

SPECIAL EQUIPMENT: Craft knife.

ADDITIONAL MATERIALS: Pink soutache braid ¼" wide, 5⁄8 yard; flat cord 1⁄8" wide, 2¼ yards; or narrow pink satin ribbon, 5⁄8 yard. White lace trim with scalloped edge ¾" wide, ½ yard. Thin white paper.

FINISHING: Trace heart onto thin white paper; cut out along marked lines for backing. Set aside. *Optional:* Following chart and directions for large card, cut out eyelets and weave ribbon through them. *Or* divide flat cord into 3 equal lengths and braid flatly. Glue braid around heart, following path of eyelets on chart. Begin at bottom and when you have returned to this starting point, use 2½" of the braid to make a loop, inserting end underneath to butt opposite end. Fold remaining ribbon or braid in half and glue ends to back of heart at top for hanging loop. Starting and ending at center top, glue straight edge of lace trim neatly around heart; cover edges. Glue backing in place.

CANDY BASKET

ADDITIONAL MATERIALS: White sewing thread. Bright pink satin picot-edged ribbon ¼" wide, ½ yard. White lace trim with scalloped edge ¾" wide, 3⁄8 yard.

DIRECTIONS: Plan and pencil the following rectangles on perforated paper: two 4½" × 4" for front and back, two 1⅜" × 2⅝" for sides, one 1¼" × 1⅜" for bottom, and one ¼" × 9" for handle. Cut out pieces. Baste center lines on front only. Work by following General Directions and chart for Candy Basket. Mark cutting outlines of front and back pieces, following dotted line on chart; cut out along marked lines.

FINISHING: Following Assembly Diagram, use 1 strand of white sewing thread to join matching edges of front and sides with overcast stitches; arch sides gently to fit curve of front. In same manner, join back to sides, then join bottom to front, back, and sides. Glue handle ends to front and back at center top; handle ends should overlap front and back by ¼". Glue straight edge of lace inside edge of top rim all around. Cut ribbon in half, make a bow with each piece, and glue to base of handle on front and back.

STATIONERY HOLDER

ADDITIONAL MATERIALS: White evenweave fabric (18-count), 5″×7″ piece. Light blue cotton fabric 36″ wide, ⅝ yard. White lace trim 1″ wide, 1 yard. Pink flat cord or soutache braid ⅛″ wide, 4½ yards. White, pink, and light blue sewing thread.

DIRECTIONS: See "Cross-Stitch Basics," page 74. Prepare evenweave fabric as directed. Fold fabric in quarters to locate center; mark fabric thread with pin. Place fabric with shorter edges at sides. Work flower-basket design, following chart and color key. Use 2 strands of floss throughout and work cross-stitches and backstitches over 1 "square" of fabric threads. Work all cross-stitches first; begin at pin with stitch indicated by arrows on chart. Then work backstitches and sprinkle French knots on top of areas covered with light loden-green cross-stitches. (See pages 75–77 for stitch details.) Press fabric, turning edges ¼″ to wrong side.

Cut two 10½″×31½″ rectangles from light blue fabric, with edges along the grain. On each rectangle, fold short ends up 7¾″, toward center of right side; press. Unfold 1 rectangle, leaving creases. With handle of basket toward center, center evenweave fabric on right side of one inside panel. Using white thread, slip-stitch evenweave in place along turned edges. Cut pink cord into 3 equal lengths and braid flatly. Beginning at one corner and using pink thread, slip-stitch braid over edges of evenweave rectangle; at each corner, make a small loop. When you reach the corner where you began, make a final loop, trim ends, and tuck underneath; stitch to secure. Beginning at a corner, pin lace trim all around, ⅛″ from braid. Slip-stitch in place along inside edge; gather edges tightly at each corner.

Refold short edges of blue fabric toward center along same creases. Stitch along long edges, making ¼″ seams and creating a pocket at each short end. Repeat on second rectangle for lining. Clip corners. Turn first rectangle to right side; press. Insert lining pocket into lining. Turn all raw edges ¼″ to inside, pin together, and slip-stitch. Press.

LARGE CARD

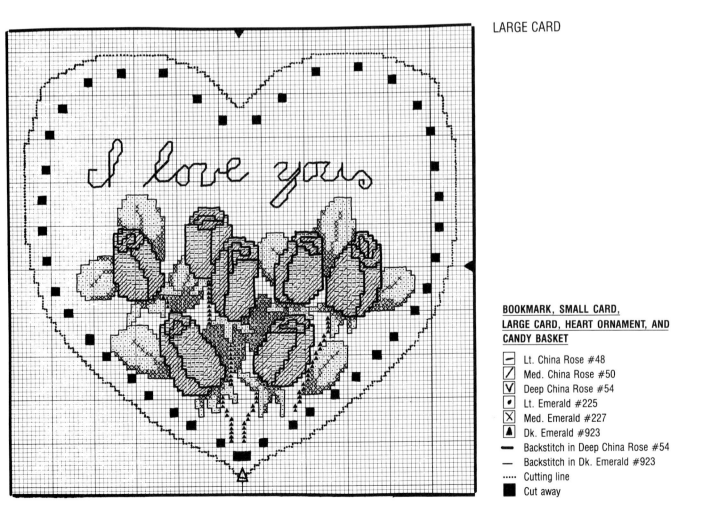

BOOKMARK, SMALL CARD, LARGE CARD, HEART ORNAMENT, AND CANDY BASKET

⌐	Lt. China Rose #48
╱	Med. China Rose #50
V	Deep China Rose #54
•	Lt. Emerald #225
X	Med. Emerald #227
▲	Dk. Emerald #923
—	Backstitch in Deep China Rose #54
—	Backstitch in Dk. Emerald #923
.....	Cutting line
■	Cut away

HEART ORNAMENT

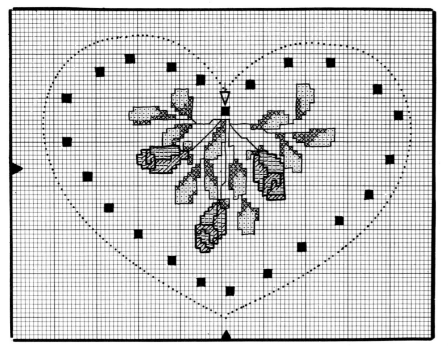

BOOKMARK

SMALL CARD

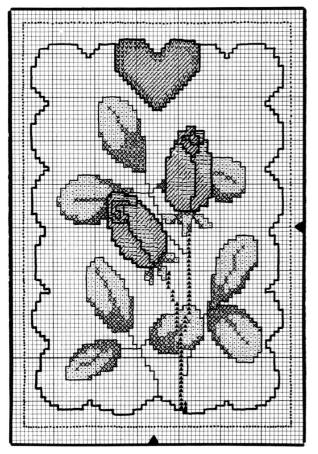

58

STATIONERY HOLDER

- **:** Lt. China Rose #48
- **/** Med. China Rose #50
- **△** Lt. Emerald #225
- **▲** Med. Emerald #227
- **X** Lt. Loden Green #259
- **O** Lt. Nutmeg #361
- **•** Med. Desert Brown #373
- **▬** Backstitch in Deep China Rose #54
- **▬** Backstitch in Dk. Desert Brown #375
- **---** Backstitch in Dk. Emerald #923
- **◯** French Knot in Med. China Rose #50

STATIONERY HOLDER

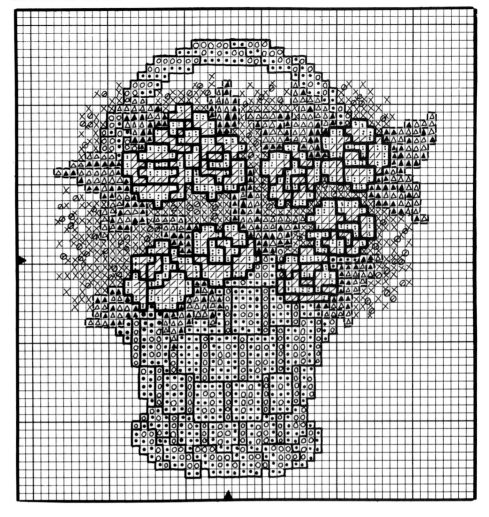

CANDY BASKET

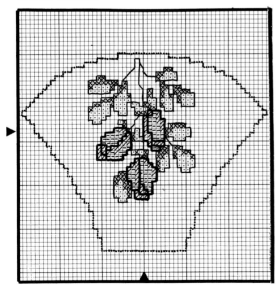

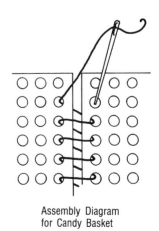

Assembly Diagram
for Candy Basket

Flower-Twined Alphabet Sampler

The alphabet and borders on this detailed sampler are cross-stitched first, then each letter is embellished with tiny blooms worked with French knots, bullion, and satin stitches. By themselves, the posy-trimmed initials will personalize gifts and clothing.

SIZE: Design area, about 10¼″ × 13″.

EQUIPMENT: Ruler. Masking tape. Straight pins. Embroidery hoop. Scissors. Tapestry needle. Iron.

MATERIALS: White Aida cloth (14-count), 16″ × 18″ piece. Susan Bates/Anchor 6-strand embroidery floss, 1 skein of each color listed in color key unless otherwise indicated in parentheses. Frame with rabbet opening at least 12″ × 14″. Sturdy cardboard to fit frame.

Med. Carnation #27	Lt. Spruce #206
Dk. Carnation #29	Med. Spruce #208
Med. China Rose #50	Dk. Spruce #210
Dk. China Rose #52	Med. Citrus #302
Deep China Rose #54	Citrus #303
Lt. Orchid #85	Med. Mint Green #204
Orchid #86	Dk. Melon #330
Med. Orchid #87	
Lt. Sapphire #159	
Med. Sapphire #161 (2)	
Med. Jonquil #295	

DIRECTIONS: See "Cross-Stitch Basics," page 74. Prepare Aida fabric as directed. Fold Aida in quarters to locate center; mark fabric thread with pin. Place Aida with longer edges at sides. Measure 6¼" up from center for placement of first stitch; mark with pin (remove first pin). Place fabric in hoop.

Work alphabet and border designs in cross-stitch, following chart and color key and beginning at pin with first border stitch (indicated by arrow on chart). Use 2 strands of floss in needle and work each cross-stitch over 1 "square" of fabric threads.

When all cross-stitch has been completed, work additional embroidery with 3 strands of floss in needle (see page 00 for stitch details). Outline flower at center top and heart at center bottom in backstitch, using dark carnation floss. Use medium mint green to work stems and to outline leaves on alphabet flowers in backstitch; fill in leaves with matching padded satin stitch. Referring to color photograph, work large flowers on alphabet in bullion knots, using shades of carnation, rose, melon, orchid, citrus, and jonquil. Work matching French knots for flower buds and contrasting French knots for flower centers.

When all embroidery has been completed, remove fabric from hoop; press. Finish and mount piece, following directions in "Cross-Stitch Basics." Frame sampler as desired.

CELEBRATION GIFTS

Momentous occasions call for out-of-the-ordinary gifts. Here are some wonderful presents to craft with care and offer with love anytime you want to commemorate one of life's special events.

Commemorative Wedding Sampler

Bestow this blessing upon your favorite newlyweds. The center scene is mounted in a personalized sampler bearing the joyous message, a coordinating border, and the date of the happy event. The choice of trimming? White lace, of course.

SIZE: Design area about 10″ × 14″.

EQUIPMENT: Graph paper. Thin cardboard. Mat knife. Cutting board. Hot glue gun. Masking tape.

MATERIALS: Aida cloth (14-count), 15″ × 19″ piece white; 6½″ × 8″ piece light blue. Susan Bates/Anchor 6-strand embroidery floss, one 8-meter skein of each color listed in color key. Pregathered white lace trim ½″ wide, 2¼ yards. Purchased frame (ours has an 11½″ × 15½″ opening). Two pieces white mat board to fit frame. Duct tape.

DIRECTIONS: Planning: Before embroidering, plan your lettering on graph paper. Chart names and date in 3 lines, using alphabets given and leaving 1 (or sometimes 2) squares between letters. Count number of squares in each line (including spaces) and write total next to it. On another area of graph paper, draw a vertical line. Draw 3 horizontal lines crossing vertical line, spaced 10 squares apart. Transfer your lettering to horizontal lines, centering so half the squares are on each side of vertical line. Place bride's name on top line, following by groom's name, then date.

Outer Section: See "Cross-Stitch Basics," page 74. Prepare Aida pieces as directed, basting center lines. Place white piece with longer edges at sides. Measure 3¾″ in from right edge along horizontal basted line; mark fabric square with pin for first stitch. Work lower half of sampler as charted, beginning with cross-stitch indicated by arrow. Use 2 strands of floss for all work; use dark blue floss to backstitch verse. Work chart in reverse for top half of border, omitting center (starred) horizontal row. When border has been completed, work dark blue

lettering in upper space as planned by matching vertical line on your chart to vertical basted line on fabric and leaving 8 Aida squares between bottom of border and top of capital letters in bride's name.

Inner Section: Place light blue Aida piece with longer edges at sides. Measure 2″ in and 2″ down from upper right corner; mark square with pin for first stitch. Using 2 strands of floss, work figures and background in cross-stitch as charted. Continuing with 2 strands, backstitch to outline veil in white, gown and shoes in medium blue; work streamers in medium green. Outline pants and inner jacket in dark blue, bowtie in dark rose. Make dark rose straight-stitch mouths and medium blue French knot eyes. Dot bushes (see dots indicated on chart) with French knot buds, yellow on left, light rose on right.

FINISHING: Draw 4⅜″ × 5⅞″ oval on thin cardboard. Center oval on wrong side of white outer section and trace. Cut away center to ½″ inside traced line.

Cut mat board to fit frame. Trace oval pattern onto center of mat board; cut along marked line. Center board over wrong side of white section; turn inner edge of fabric onto cardboard, clipping as necessary and taping securely in place. Hot-glue lace around opening, lapping gathered edge over cardboard. Turn outer edge of fabric onto cardboard and tape in place, checking right side to be sure fabric is taut and design is straight. Hot-glue remaining lace around inner edges of frame as shown in photograph. Secure white piece in frame. Tape inner blue section tautly to another piece of mat board, centering it. Insert and secure piece in frame.

ALPHABETS AND NUMBERS

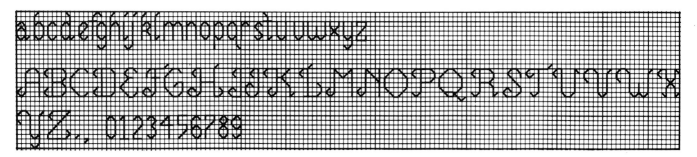

64

May joy and peace surround you,
Contentment latch your door,
And happiness be with you now
And bless you evermore.

INNER SECTION

−	Lt. Green #206
∕	Med. Green #210
✕	Lavender #104
=	Lt. Sand #368
▲	Dk. Sand #370
•.	Yellow #300
∟	Flesh #4146
╬	Lt. Gray #397
╲	Med. Gray #399
•	White #2
∴	Lt. Rose #24
∨	Dk. Rose #68
∣	Lt. Blue #144
┖	Med. Blue #977
■	Dk. Blue #979

Presents for Baby

Baby-soft colors and cute-as-a-button bunnies give these infant gifts their endearing appeal. Rabbits tiptoe through the tulips on the adorable picture frame and hop beneath them on the cover of the baby's book. Two of them proudly show off the birth announcement on the keepsake plaque, while one sleepy-time bunny snoozes contentedly on the pastel doorknob sign.

BABY'S BOOK

SIZE: Design area, about 7¾″ × 8½″.

MATERIALS: Yellow Aida cloth (14-count), 10″ × 11″ piece. DMC 6-strand embroidery floss, 1 skein of each color listed in color key unless otherwise indicated in parentheses. Blue calico 44″ wide, ½ yard. Sewing thread to match calico. Purchased picture album, about 10″ × 12″.

DIRECTIONS: See "Cross-Stitch Basics," page 74. Prepare Aida fabric for embroidery. Place Aida right side up on flat surface with 10″ edges at top

and bottom. Measure 1¼″ down from center of top edge and mark fabric square with pin for placement of first stitch. Beginning at center top of border, work design in cross-stitch by following chart and color key. Use 3 strands of floss in embroidery needle and make each stitch over 1 square of Aida fabric. When cross-stitch has been completed, outline bunnies' bodies in backstitch using 2 strands of blue.

When all embroidery has been completed, gently press piece facedown on padded surface. Fold excess fabric on each edge to wrong side along first row of holes outside cross-stitch; press.

Cover: Measure closed picture album from front

edge around spine to back edge and from top to bottom. Add 12″ to width and 2″ to height, then cut a piece of calico to these dimensions for cover. Press side cover edges ¼″, then ¾″ to wrong side; top-stitch. Turn folded edges 5″ to right side for flaps. Stitch through flaps 1″ from top and bottom edges. With flaps still wrong side out, press top and bottom raw edges under ¼″, then ¾″; topstitch, or hem by hand. Turn flaps to inside and slip cover onto album. Center embroidery on cover front; pin in place. Remove cover. Topstitch or slip-stitch close to Aida edges.

SHH! DOORKNOB SIGN

SIZE: 8″×6″.

EQUIPMENT: Straight pins. Embroidery needle. Iron. Water-erasable pen. Scissors.

MATERIALS: Pale green Aida cloth (14-count), 2 pieces 14″×12″. DMC 6-strand embroidery floss, 1 skein of each color listed in color key unless other-wise indicated in parentheses. Pale green ribbon ⅜″ wide, 11″. Sewing thread to match fabric. Fiberfill or cotton balls for stuffing.

DIRECTIONS: See "Cross-Stitch Basics," page 74. Prepare 1 piece of Aida fabric for embroidery. Locate center of prepared piece and mark fabric square with pin for first stitch. With long fabric edges at top and bottom, work design in cross-stitch, following chart and color key. Use 3 strands of floss in embroidery needle and make each stitch over 1 square of Aida fabric. Fill in bunny body with white cross-stitch; leave background plain. Work backstitch in pink for eye and light blue for body details.

When all embroidery has been completed, gently press piece facedown on padded surface. Using water-erasable pen and following chart, mark sign outline around embroidery for front piece. Cut out front, adding ¼″ seam allowance all around. Cut matching back piece from remaining Aida.

With raw edges even and ribbon against fabric, pin ribbon ends to right side of sign front where indicated by X's on chart. Stitch sign front and back together, leaving an opening for turning; turn to right side. Stuff sign until plump. Slip-stitch opening closed.

KEEPSAKE PLAQUE

SIZE: Design area, about 7½″×9½″.

EQUIPMENT: Straight pins. Tapestry needle. Graph paper. Iron. Sewing needle.

MATERIALS: White Aida cloth (14-count), 14″×17″ piece. DMC 6-strand embroidery floss, 1 skein of each color listed in color key unless otherwise indicated in parentheses. Pink ribbon ⅛″ wide, 8″.

DIRECTIONS: See "Cross-Stitch Basics," page 74. Prepare fabric for embroidery. Place piece right side up on flat surface with short edges at top and bottom. Measure 3¾″ down from center of top edge and mark fabric with pin for placement of first stitch.

Beginning at center top of border with uppermost gold stitch in bouquet (arrow), work design in cross-stitch by following sampler chart and color key. Use 3 strands of floss in tapestry needle and make each stitch over 1 square of Aida fabric. Disregard heavy lines on chart. **Name and date:** Chart desired name and date on graph paper by following alphabet chart: Leave 1 blank square between adjacent characters; 5 squares between first and last names; 3 squares between month and day; 1, 2, or 3 squares between comma (following day) and year. (If either line exceeds 77 squares in width, use first name only, use nickname, or abbreviate month.) Center name above date and leave 6 squares between lines. Mark center of top row of squares on name line for first stitch. Work name and date in cross-stitch, using 3 strands of blue floss and beginning 5 squares below heart (asterisk).

When cross-stitch has been completed, work backstitch with 3 strands of floss by following heavy lines on chart; make each straight or diagonal stitch over 1 fabric square: Work bouquet stems with green; bows and bunnies' mouths with bright pink; inside and outside of large heart outline with light pink; bunny bodies and eyebrows with blue.

FINISHING: When all embroidery has been completed, gently press piece facedown on padded surface. Cut ribbon into two 4″ lengths. Tie a bow with each length; press flat. Using 1 strand of light pink floss in sewing needle and making invisible stitches, tack a bow to each side of large heart as shown in photograph.

Mount and frame sampler as desired.

BUNNY FRAME

SIZE: About 7¾″×10″

EQUIPMENT: Straight pins. Embroidery needle. Iron. Ruler. Craft knife. Scissors. Pencil.

MATERIALS: White Aida cloth (14-count), 11″×13″ piece. DMC 6-strand embroidery floss, 1 skein of each color listed in color key. Scrap of white cotton fabric. White and dark sewing threads. Sturdy cardboard. Batting. White craft glue.

DIRECTIONS: See "Cross-Stitch Basics," page 74. Prepare Aida fabric for embroidery. With short edges of Aida at top and bottom, measure 1⅝" up from center bottom and mark fabric square with pin. Beginning at center bottom of outer border, work design in cross-stitch by following chart and color key. Use 3 strands of floss in needle and make each stitch over 1 square of Aida fabric. Work bottom right quarter of frame as shown on chart. To work bottom left quarter, work chart in reverse, omitting starred (vertical center) row. For top left quarter, work another tulip, leaving 5 squares between center top of first tulip and stem of second tulip. Work a second heart, leaving 3 squares between center of second tulip and heart. For a second bunny, work inner ear, counting 21 squares up from center of heart and 2 squares to the right for first stitch. Work remainder of frame top as for bottom. Work another heart and tulip to complete top right quarter. When cross-stitch has been completed, outline bunnies with backstitch using 3 strands of blue floss.

When all embroidery has been completed, gently press piece facedown on padded surface. Using dark thread in needle, baste along inside and outside edges of embroidered frame (1, 2, or 3 rows beyond inner and outer green borders as desired). Measure embroidered frame between bastings and mark a frame on cardboard with same dimensions. Carefully cut out cardboard frame with craft knife; use as pattern to cut matching piece of batting. Glue batting to cardboard. Cut 7" × 9" piece of white fabric for facing. With right sides together, center facing over embroidered piece; stitch close to inner basting line; remove basting. Cut away both layers of center rectangle to within ¼" of stitching line; snip into corners. With embroidered fabric on batting side and clipped seam allowance on cardboard side, pull facing through cardboard opening; seam should line up with inner edge of cardboard frame. Fold all edges to back of frame and glue in place, mitering corners. Remove outer basting.

For back, mark rectangle on cardboard same size as front; cut out. Cut three 1"-wide spacer strips from cardboard, two 9½" long for sides and one 7½" long for bottom. Glue strips to back of frame; let dry. Spread glue on strips; press front and back frame pieces together, matching edges.

Following diagram, cut easel stand from cardboard. Using craft knife, score (do not cut through) stand along dash line for spine; fold along scoring so that scoring is outside; spread glue on spine. Position spine, glued side down, on frame back so that bottom edge of stand is flush with center bottom edge of frame; let dry.

SHH! DOORKNOB SIGN

EASEL STAND

1"

5"

3½"

⅜"

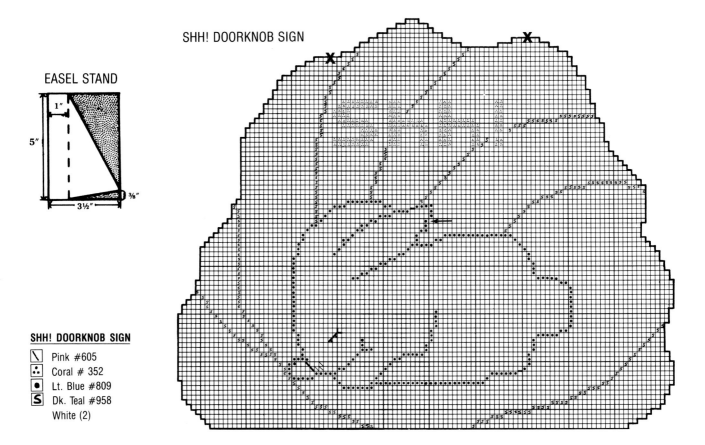

SHH! DOORKNOB SIGN

⟍	Pink #605
∴	Coral # 352
●	Lt. Blue #809
S	Dk. Teal #958
	White (2)

BABY'S BOOK

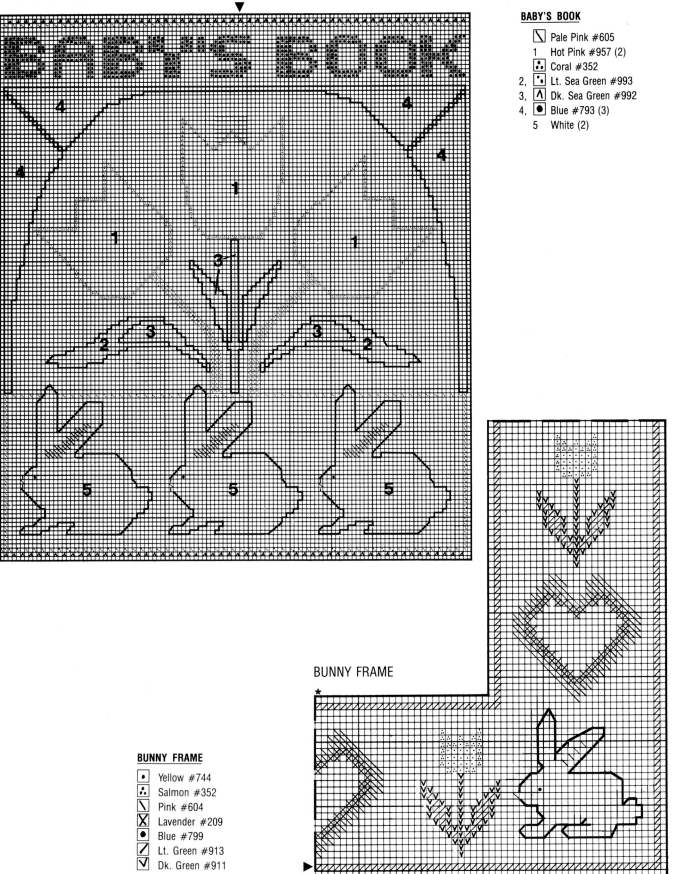

BUNNY FRAME

KEEPSAKE PLAQUE

Gold #752
Coral #352
Brt. Pink #603
Lt. Pink #605 (2)
Blue #799
Aqua #598
Teal #597
Green #910

Season's Greetings
Christmas Crafts

You'll cherish these holiday accessories for their elegant simplicity. Cross-stitched wreaths and candles adorn a miniature trinket box, a tiny vine wreath plaque, and a festive table runner.

CHRISTMAS WREATH AND BOX

SIZE: Design area for each, about 2⅜″ square.

EQUIPMENT: For Embroidery: Straight pins. Embroidery needle. **For Vine Wreath:** Hot-glue gun. Air-soluble marking pen. Compass. Scissors. **For Box:** Compass. Scissors.

MATERIALS: For Each: Ecru Aida cloth (11-count), 6″ square piece. Susan Bates/Anchor embroidery floss, one 8-meter skein of each color listed in color key (will be enough for several embroideries). **For Vine Wreath:** Purchased 4½″-diameter vine wreath. Green satin ribbon ⅛″ wide, ½

yard. Fusible Pellon.® **For Box:** Purchased rosewood trinket box with 3½″-diameter cover insert.

DIRECTIONS: Embroidery: See "Cross-Stitch Basics," page 74. Overcast raw edges of Aida to prevent raveling. Fold Aida in quarters to determine center square of fabric. Counting from center square, determine placement of first stitch as follows: wreath design, 14 squares up and 3 squares to the left; poinsettia design, 15 squares up and 5 squares to the left; candle design, 13 squares up; mark square with pin for first stitch. (Any of the 3 signs can be used for vine wreath or box.) Using two strands of floss in needle and referring to chart and color key, work designed design in cross-stitch.

When motif has been completed, work solid lines on chart in backstitch; use 2 strands of dark brown floss in needle.

FINISHING: Vine Wreath: Fuse embroidery to Pellon® following manufacturer's directions. With point of compass on center stitch, carefully draw a 4"-diameter circle around motif. Cut out on marked circle. Place piece right side up on flat work surface. Apply hot glue all around edge of circle. Place vine wreath on top of embroidery, centering carefully, and press firmly until glue sets. Tie green ribbon into bow and hot-glue to top of wreath. Secure streamers to wreath with glue as necessary.
Box: Draw 4"-diameter circle around embroidery as for vine-wreath embroidery and cut out. Insert embroidery into box cover following manufacturer's directions.

TABLE RUNNER

SIZE: 16½" × 62½".

MATERIALS: Zweigart ecru "Bondeno" 100% polyacrylic fabric (article #7532) 71" wide, ⅝–¾ yard (see Source Guide, page 78). Susan Bates/Anchor embroidery floss, one 8-meter skein of each color listed in color key unless otherwise noted in parentheses
Note: "Bondeno" fabric has a woven-in windowpane design. To make runner, you will need a piece at least 65" × 22", with a design area 8 blocks long × 2 blocks wide centered within.

DIRECTIONS: Embroidery: See "Cross-Stitch Basics," page 74. Overcast raw edges of fabric to prevent raveling. Lay fabric on flat surface, right side up, with short edges at sides. Use 6 strands of floss in needle and referring to charts, color key, and placement directions below, work the 3 designs in cross-stitch over 1 "square" of 3 horizontal and 1 vertical fabric threads. When each motif has been completed, work solid lines on chart in backstitch using 6 strands of dark-brown floss.

To Place First Stitch: Each block is 31 squares wide × 31 squares long. Start at top left corner of block to be worked. For wreath, count 13 squares across, 3 squares down; for poinsettia, 11 squares across, 2 squares down; for candle, 16 squares across, 3 squares down.

To Place Motifs: Starting at top left block, embroider top row as follows: wreath, 1 block blank, poinsettia, 1 block blank, candle, 1 block blank, wreath, 1 block blank. Embroider bottom row from left to right as follows: 1 block blank, candle, 1 block blank, wreath, 1 block blank, poinsettia, 1 block blank, candle.

FINISHING: Hand-wash piece if necessary and press on well-padded surface. Lay piece on flat surface, right side up, with short edges at sides. Using a ruler and air-soluble or water-erasable marking pen, draw 2 vertical lines 2¾" and 4¼" from inner left edge of 2 blocks on left side of piece; repeat for right side of piece. Set sewing machine for fine stitch length and straight-stitch along the inner lines. Cut fabric along outer lines. Ravel fabric threads to machine stitching, forming self-fringe. To finish long edges, measure and mark 2 lines 3½" from outer edges of blocks. Cut fabric along lines, then turn each edge ¾" to wrong side twice; topstitch through all thicknesses ⅜" from fold.

WREATH

CANDLE

POINSETTIA

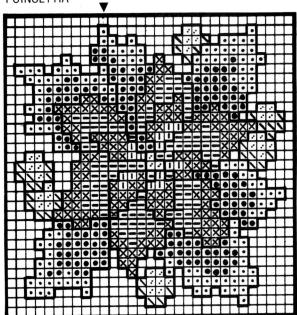

	Lt. Red #35
X	Red #46 (3)
—	Dk. Red #19
·	Lt. Green #243 (3)
●	Dk. Green #246 (4)
·'	Lt. Gold #305
\	Dk. Gold #307
	Dk. Brown #380 (3)

CROSS-STITCH BASICS

Embroidery Tips

THREADING THE NEEDLE
To thread yarn or floss through the needle eye, double it over the end of the needle and slip it off, holding it tightly as close as possible to the fold. Push the eye of the needle down over the folded end and pull the yarn through.

TO BEGIN A STITCH
Start your embroidery with two or three tiny running stitches toward the starting point, then take a tiny backstitch and begin. Do not make knots when beginning or ending stitches.

TO END A COLOR
Fasten off the thread when ending each motif rather than carrying it to another motif. Pass the end of the thread through the last few stitches on the wrong side or take a few tiny backstitches.

TO REMOVE EMBROIDERY
When a mistake has been made, run a needle, eye first, under the stitches. Pull the embroidery away from the fabric; cut carefully with scissors pressed hard against the needle. Pick out the cut portion of the embroidery. Catch any loose ends of the remaining stitches on the back by pulling the ends under the stitches with a crochet hook.

Finishing Techniques

TO PREPARE FOR FINISHING
When your embroidered piece has been completed, finish off the back neatly by running the ends into the back of the work and clipping off any excess strands. If wool embroidery is not really soiled but needs just a little freshening, simply brushing over the surface with a clean cloth dipped in carbon tetrachloride or another good cleaning fluid may be satisfactory. This will brighten and restore colors to their original look. If the fabric is soiled, wash it gently. Embroideries made of colorfast threads and washable fabrics can be laundered without fear of harming them. Wash the fabric with a mild soap or detergent and warm water, swishing it through the water gently—do not rub. Rinse in clear water without wringing or squeezing. When the fabric has been completely rinsed, lift it from the water and lay it on a clean towel; lay another towel on top and roll up loosely. When the embroidery is sufficiently dry, press it as described below.

Better results will be obtained by blocking rather than pressing an embroidered piece for a picture or hanging. However, articles that are hemmed, such as tablecloths or runners, should be pressed; blocking would damage the edge of the fabric. To press your embroidered piece, use a well-padded surface and a steam iron or a regular iron and a damp cloth. Embroideries that have been worked in a frame will require very little pressing. If the embroidery was done in the hand, it will no doubt be quite wrinkled and may need dampening. Sprinkle it to dampen and roll it loosely in a clean towel. Embroidery should always be pressed lightly, to prevent the stitching from being flattened into the fabric. Place the embroidered piece facedown on the padded surface and press from the center outward. For embroidery that is raised from the surface of the background, use extra-thick, soft padding, such as a thick blanket.

After blocking or pressing, an embroidered picture should be mounted immediately to prevent creasing.

TO BLOCK
Using a needle and colorfast thread, follow the thread of the linen and take ¼" stitches to mark guidelines around the entire picture, designating the exact area where the picture will fit into the rabbet of the frame. The border of plain linen extending beyond the embroidery in a framed picture is approximately 1¼" at the sides and top and 1½" at the bottom. In order to have sufficient linen around the embroidered design for blocking and mounting, 3" or 4" of linen should be left around the embroidered section. Now, matching the corners, obtain the exact centers of the four sides and mark these centers with a few stitches.

If the picture is soiled, it should be blocked immediately after washing. In preparation, cover a drawing board or soft wood breadboard with a piece of brown paper held in place with thumbtacks and draw the exact original size of the linen on the brown paper. Be sure the linen isn't pulled beyond its original size when the measurements are taken. (Embroidery sometimes pulls linen slightly out of shape.) Check the drawn rectangle to make sure the corners are square.

Wash the embroidery; let it drip for a minute. Place the embroidery right side up on the brown paper inside the guidelines and tack down the four corners. Tack the centers of four sides. Continue to stretch the linen to its original size by tacking all around the sides, dividing and subdividing the spaces between the tacks already placed. This procedure is followed until there is a solid border of thumbtacks around the entire edge. In cross-stitch pictures, if stitches were not worked exactly even on the thread of the linen, it may be necessary to remove some of the tacks and pull part of the embroidery into a straight line. Use a ruler as a guide for straightening the lines of stitches. Hammer in the tacks or they will pop out as the linen dries. Allow the embroidery to dry thoroughly.

TO MOUNT
Cut a piece of heavy white cardboard about ⅛" smaller all around than the rabbet size of the frame to be used. Stretch the embroidery over the cardboard, using the same general procedure outlined for blocking the piece. Following the thread guidelines, use pins to attach the four corners of the embroidery to the mounting board. Pins are placed at the centers of the sides, and the embroidery is then gradually stretched into position until there is a border of pins completely around the picture—about ¼" apart. When you are satisfied that the design is even, drive the pins into the cardboard edge with a hammer. If a pin does not go in straight, it should be removed and reinserted. The edges of the linen can either be pasted or taped down on the wrong side of the cardboard or caught with long zigzag stitches. Embroidered pictures can be framed with glass over them if desired.

Cross-Stitch How-to's

To prevent the fabric from raveling, bind all raw edges with masking tape, whipstitch edges by hand, or machine-stitch ⅛" in from all edges. Work the embroidery in a frame or hoop to keep the fabric taut; move the hoop as needed. Cut the floss or yarn into 18" lengths. To begin a strand, leave an end on the back and work over it to secure; to end, run the needle under four or five stitches on the back of the work.

Each symbol on the chart represents one cross-stitch. Different symbols represent different colors. When working cross-stitches, work all underneath stitches in one direction and all top stitches in the opposite direction, making sure all threads lie smooth and flat; allow the needle to hang freely from the work occasionally to untwist the floss. Make crosses touch by inserting the needle in the same hole used for the adjacent stitch (see illustration).

Several different ways to do cross-stitch are described below. All yield equally good results if care is taken to make sure that the strands of threads or yarn lie smooth and flat.

Four Methods of Cross-Stitching

MONK'S OR AIDA CLOTH
The design can follow the mesh of a coarse, flat-weave fabric, such as monk's cloth. Here the design can be worked from a chart simply by counting each square of fabric for one stitch.

GINGHAM
A checked material, such as gingham, can be used as a guide for cross-stitch. Crosses are made over checks, following a chart.

EVENWEAVE FABRIC
The threads of an evenweave fabric, such as sampler linen, can be counted and each cross-stitch made the same size.

PENELOPE CANVAS
Penelope (or cross-stitch) canvas is basted to the fabric on which the design is to be embroidered. First, center the canvas over the fabric, making sure that the horizontal and vertical threads of the canvas and fabric match; then make lines of basting diagonally in both directions and around the sides of the canvas. The design is then worked by making crosses as shown. Each stitch is taken over

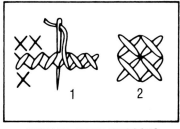

HOW TO MAKE CROSSES

the double mesh of canvas diagonally and through the fabric, being careful not to catch the canvas.

When the design has been completed, the basting is removed and the horizontal threads of the canvas are carefully drawn out, one strand at a time, followed by the vertical threads. The finished cross-stitch design remains on the fabric.

Penelope canvas is available in meshes of several sizes. Choose finer sizes for smaller designs; larger sizes are suitable for coarse work in wool.

Embroidery Stitch Details

BACKSTITCH

OUTLINE STITCH

RUNNING STITCH

STRAIGHT STITCH

HALF CROSS-STITCH

FRENCH KNOT

SATIN STITCH

PADDED SATIN STITCH

BULLION STITCH

Sewing Hints

TO JOIN FABRIC PIECES

Pin the pieces together with the right sides facing each other and the raw edges even unless otherwise directed. Machine-stitch on marked lines with matching thread, making ¼″ seams unless otherwise directed; ease in any fullness where necessary. Press seams open after stitching unless otherwise specified. When joining patch pieces, press seams to one side, under the darker color. Clip into the seam allowance at curves and across corners; turn the piece to the right side when directed and poke out the corners with a knitting needle. Assemble and finish pieces as directed.

TO MAKE A HEM

Press the fabric edge ¼″ to the wrong side. Turn under again to the desired depth; press. Topstitch by machine or slip-stitch by hand.

TO MAKE A PILLOW

Cut out the pillow front from the fabric, needle-point canvas, felt, etc., as specified. Cut the pillow back the same size. If desired, add ruffle or welting as directed below, then assemble the pillow: Stitch the pillow front and back together, making ½″ seams and leaving an opening in one side for turn-

ing. Turn the pillow to the right side. Stuff firmly with fiberfill or insert the pillow form. Turn in the raw edges and slip-stitch the opening closed.

FOR A RUFFLE

Cut the fabric strip for the ruffle as directed, piecing together as necessary. Stitch ruffle ends together; press the seam open. Fold the ruffle in half lengthwise right side out; press. Using a long basting stitch, gather the ruffle ½″ from the raw edges to fit around the pillow front. Stitch the ruffle to the right side of the pillow front.

Patchwork How-to's

TO MAKE PATCHWORK TEMPLATES

Draw and label the patterns on the graph paper, using a ruler to mark straight lines; do not cut out yet. Glue the paper pattern to a piece of cardboard; let dry. Cut out on the marked lines for the templates.

TO MARK PATCH PIECES

Place the template on the wrong side of the fabric with parallel edges, right angles, or one straight edge on the straight grain. Mark around the template with a sharp pencil held at an outward angle. Mark the specified number of pieces needed on one fabric at one time, leaving ½" between pieces.

TO CUT PATTERN/PATCHWORK PIECES
Cut out fabric pieces ¼" beyond the marked lines (stitching lines) for the seam allowance unless otherwise directed. If you're cutting additional pieces without patterns, do not add the seam allowance; it is included in the dimensions given. To prevent knit-backed or loosely woven fabric from raveling, zigzag-stitch all raw edges as necessary.

PIECING
To join two patch pieces by hand, place them together, with the right sides facing, matching angles and marked lines; pin. Thread a sharp needle with an 18" length of sewing thread. Begin with a small knot, then stitch along the marked seam line with tiny running stitches, ending with a few backstitches. Try to make 8 to 10 running stitches per inch. As you join the pieces, press the seams to one side; open seams tend to weaken construction.

To join the pieces by machine, set the machine for 10 stitches per inch and join as you would for hand piecing.

Source Guide

Write for direct mail-order information or name of store near you.

Anchor: See Susan Bates.
Charles Craft, Inc., P.O. Box 1049, Laurinburg, NC 28353; 919-844-3521.
DMC: Available in needlework shops or by mail from Craft Gallery Ltd., P.O. Box 8319, Salem, MA 01971-8319. For information, write to: DMC, Port Kearny Building #10, South Kearny, NJ 07032-0650.
Ribband: Available in needlework shops. For information, write to: Leisure Arts, P.O. Box 5595, Little Rock, AR 72215; 800-643-8030; Arkansas residents call 800-632-7357.
Sudberry House, Four Mile and Colton Roads, Box 895, Old Lyme, CT 06371.
Sunshine Station, P.O. Drawer 2388, Hickory, NC 28603; 704-324-4445.
Susan Bates/Anchor: Available in needlework shops. For information, write to: Susan Bates, 212 Middlesex Avenue, Chester, CT 06412.
Zweigart: Available in needlework shops. For information, write to: Rosemary Drysdale, 80 Long Lane, East Hampton, NY 11937.

Index

All of us at Meredith® Press are dedicated to offering you, our customer, the best books we can create. We are particularly concerned that all of the instructions for making the projects are clear and accurate. We welcome your comments and would like to hear any suggestions you may have. Please address your correspondence to Customer Service Department, Meredith® Press, Meredith Corporation, 150 East 52nd Street, New York, NY 10022.